The Ultimate Shell Seeker's Guide

The Ultimate Shell Seeker's Guide

Building a Better Beachcombing Strategy

Ashley Oliphant

The University of Georgia Press Athens

A Wormsloe
FOUNDATION
nature book

All images are by the author except the following, for which the author thanks the photographers: Hemingway Water Shuttle (p. 90), Beth Yarbrough (p. 97), Cheryl Carrier (p. 223), and Chris Oliphant (p. 280).

Published by the University of Georgia Press
Athens, Georgia 30602
www.ugapress.org

Designed by Erin Kirk
Set in Miller Text
Printed and bound by Martin Book Management
The paper in this book meets the guidelines for permanence and durability of the Committee on Production Guidelines for Book Longevity of the Council on Library Resources.

Printed in Korea
30 29 28 27 26 P 5 4 3 2 1

EU Authorized Representative
Easy Access System Europe—Mustamäe tee 50, 10621 Tallinn, Estonia, gpsr.requests@easproject.com

Library of Congress Cataloging-in-Publication Data

Names: Oliphant, Ashley, 1978– author
Title: The ultimate shell seeker's guide : building a better beachcombing strategy / Ashley Oliphant.
Description: Athens : The University of Georgia Press, [2026] | Series: Wormsloe foundation nature books | Includes bibliographical references and index.
Identifiers: LCCN 2025043638 | ISBN 9780820374741 paperback
Subjects: LCSH: Shells—Identification | Beachcombing
Classification: LCC QL405 .O448 2025
LC record available at https://lccn.loc.gov/2025043638

It's for him. It's always going to be for him.

And to the late great Jimmy Buffett:
Your books and lyrics gave me permission
to chase the tides and dream really big.
Sail on, sailor.

Contents

Preface xiii

It All Starts with Your Attitude 1
Exploring for Yourself 7

Shelling Strategy

Plotting Your Moves in Advance 11
Identifying Shell Beds and Wrack Lines 12
Reading the Tide Charts 17
Picking the Best Moon 24
Charting Wind Directions 27
Capitalizing on Fall Storms and Strong Winter Currents 30
Recognizing the Advantage of Unpleasant Weather 34
Studying Shells as Hunting Preparation 37
Researching and Troubleshooting 40
Tracking Beach Renourishment Projects 42
Choosing Your Location 45

Hunting Like a Boss

Getting Up Early 111
Reading the Beach 113
Shelling Speed 117
Putting in the Time 120
Walking the Shelling Grid 122
Watching the Waves for Rolling Shells 124
Digging, Sifting, and Raking 125
Maximizing the Benefit of Moving Water 128
Identifying Pusher and Sucker Tides 131
Recognizing the Competition 133
Wading to Sandbars 135
Searching Tidal Pools, Tree Roots, Berm Walls, and Rock Jetties 136
Finding a Honey Hole 140
Beach Hopping 142
Assessing Water Clarity 144
Hunting at Night 146
Putting All of These Strategies Together: A Keewaydin Island Story 149

Continuing to Build Your Skills

Training Your Eye 155
Hunting Inland Rivers and Creeks 157
Taking Shelling Excursions 160
Staying Safe on the Beach 165
Monitoring Weather Conditions 171
Ethical Beachcombing and Why We Don't "Live Shell" 172
Essential Gear 177
Cleaning and Displaying Your Shells 183
The Stinky Red Tide 190
Avoiding "No-See-Ums," Chiggers, and Other Devious Bugs 192
Wedding Shells 195
Albino Shells 197

Appreciating "Mini" Shells 198
Looking Up for Sunrises and Sunsets 200
Knowing the Rules and Regulations 202
Resources and Recommended Online Forums 204

Dr. O's Bucket List Species

Junonias 213
Scotch Bonnets 216
Lion's Paws 217
Flat Scallops 218
Horse Conchs 220
Cones 222
Helmets 224
Tuns 225
Cowries 227
Caribbean Vases 228
Sundials 229
Wentletraps 230
Moon Snails 231
Olives 233
Angelwings 234
Whelks 236

Tulips 238
Nutmegs 241
Murexes 242
Tellins 245
Spiny and Leafy Jewelboxes 246
Crown Conchs 248

Other Notable Beach Finds

Shark Teeth 251
Sea Beans 253
Indigenous Artifacts 256
Military Artifacts 258
Sea Glass 260
Sea Biscuits 263
Sand Dollars 265
Sea Urchins 267
Starfish 269
Crab Shells and Legs 271
Serendipitous Treasures 273

Conclusion 279
Special Thanks 281
Works Cited 283
Index 285
About the Author 291

Turn off your ringer. Leave it all behind. There's a stillness to be found out there when you let your mind get really quiet. If you've lost touch with who you are, your best shot at finding it again is beside the ocean. Go put your toes in the sand. The answers are there.

Preface

The fact that this book is in your hands means that you are my people. Welcome to *The Ultimate Shell Seeker's Guide*, a text written specifically for you—the folks who walk two extra miles in the rain while telling themselves "Just one more shell, and I'll go home." It's for my friends who can't sleep at night because they're obsessing about what the tide might be leaving behind. It's for those dedicated beachcombers who won't be deterred on their quest for that one bucket-list shell. It's for the people who go to the beach for solace in this increasingly crazy world and find renewal for their spirits in the colors of the fading sunset.

I decided to write *The Ultimate Shell Seeker's Guide* because it's a book I would want to read if it was available to me on a store or library shelf. While there are several comprehensive guides to seashell *identification*, nobody has ever written a book that focuses on the *strategy* for finding them, mainly because that's the part the experts don't want to give away. They aren't eager to tell newcomers where their "honey holes" are or how to read the conditions to know when the ocean will give up the biggest and best shells. As I have toured nationally and interacted with thousands of beachcombers at my shelling and shark tooth hunting workshops and classes, I've realized it's that hunger for the hidden information that makes people want to attend my events and ask questions. There's a deep desire to learn but a great shortage of willing teachers.

Every person has a right to know and to learn. That's the reason I've always been open to sharing my beachcombing knowledge in whatever capacity I can. I don't take kindly to those in the seashell and fossil forums who refuse to pause for one minute to answer a novice's question and instead bark about their beaches being too full of visitors, the online chats being clogged with repetitive posts, and people taking too many seashells from the beach. Nobody owns the public beaches, every sheller (including me) was once a newcomer with "too many questions," and there are plenty of seashells on

Raise your hand if you have sand in the floorboards of your car (and maybe a little bit in your kitchen, too).

this planet to go around. By helping others find wonderful things and by teaching them to be responsible beachcombers who take care of wildlife and respect the ecosystem, I know Mother Ocean will make sure I continue to pocket my share of the treasure.

I'm so happy this book is now in print, and I vow not to hold anything back that I think might be helpful. Nobody falls asleep in Dr. O's class, so I won't throw stiff Latin species names at you, nor am I going to bog you down with exhaustive explanations about every single thing you might find on a beach. We're going to focus on grand-prize shells and how to have an awesome time finding them. My wish is that the words on these pages lead you and your family to the most spectacular seashells you can imagine. Let's go hunting!

The Ultimate Shell Seeker's Guide

It All Starts with Your Attitude

The most effective shellers are patient people who are truly grateful for every gift from the sea. They go onto the beach every day with the understanding that they'll find what they're meant to find. If someone else picks up something thrilling, these savvy beachcombers are genuinely happy. Instead of thinking "Shoot, I was just looking there" or "Why him and not me?," they celebrate with their fellow beachcomber. The truth is the once-in-a-lifetime shells find you—you don't find them. Experience proves that your turn will come sooner if you have a positive attitude along the way and don't lose patience or your ability to sincerely congratulate someone else. The key to getting full joy out of the beach experience is to be less concerned with what comes home in your shell bucket and more focused on the pleasure of the adventure. You'll do your best hunting when you have your mind in the right place. Optimistic thinking usually yields results.

It's easy to become frustrated when you see someone nearby pull up a rare seashell or shark tooth that you've always wanted for your own collection. That competitive spirit is a natural impulse among people who are drawn to a find-and-keep hobby. If you sense your irritation rising because you aren't having any success, though, remember a glum attitude will throw you right into a ditch, and that defeats the whole purpose of recreational time.

Because the ocean gives and takes as she pleases, there are going to be beach days when nobody is finding anything. The social media complaints are everywhere: "I went to the beach y'all recommended, and there was nothing there. This isn't fair." Not every beach will produce every day. You also can't command the ocean to deliver seashells, so there are times when you just have to acknowledge that today is not your day and pivot. When that happens, turn your attention to other activities that are still going to feed your spirit because every beach presents endless opportunities for that. Here are some recommendations that can help you cope with a "bad" shelling

A few years ago, I met another fossil hunter for some night hunting. Shortly after arrival, he found a three-inch great white shark tooth (which is really as big as they get). It was breathtaking. I'm not too proud to admit that I was a little jealous. I've never found a great white tooth that large, and he was hunting in an area that I had considered visiting first, but I had chosen an entry point about two miles down the beach instead. I did my best to keep my attitude in check and to focus instead on how excited my friend was about his find. Just a few minutes later, my eye zeroed in on this Indigenous spear point from the Archaic period, and I was reminded of my own advice. That tooth was intended for him, and there was a different kind of fulfillment waiting for me on down the beach.

day. These strategies can be particularly helpful if you're dealing with disappointed kids who had their hearts set on finding a specific thing.

- Switch gears and hunt for something different. If you were hoping for shells or shark teeth, look instead for sea beans, coins, fossils, crab shells, or sea glass.
- Focus on finding and observing live creatures like coquina clams burrowing in the sand.
- Watch for dolphins. They often surface just past the breaking waves.
- Walk out on a pier to spend some time around the anglers. While there, keep your eyes open for sharks in the water. You can almost always see them if you're paying attention. Early mornings are an optimal time to view them.
- See how many different species of birds you can identify.

- Pick a color (like yellow, pink, or orange) and try to put together a handful of seashells just in that color, even if they're broken.
- Experiment with beach photography. You'll learn something new every time you take pictures beside the water.
- Do some deep breathing as you walk to clear your head.
- Share some of the common shells or shark teeth you have found with other people and teach them about the species if they don't know.
- Pick up some trash to keep your local beach clean.

Most important, be willing to try again. The expert hunters didn't gain that status by being easily dissuaded by an unfavorable tide. You'll quickly learn that beachcombing is a hit-or-miss activity with no guarantees. Put on your happy pants and give it a go tomorrow.

OPPOSITE: *For centuries, sailors have extolled the virtues of not talking unnecessarily at sea. The same should apply to the beach. You'd be amazed at how much your overall attitude will improve if you spend a few hours not talking to anybody. Dauphin Island, Alabama, is the perfect place to be quiet.*

Exploring for Yourself

You bought this book to learn from someone else's experience, which is wise. There's a treasure trove of information knocking around in the heads of the seasoned beachcombers if you can get them to talk. The reason this book is necessary, though, is because many of the experts don't want to hand over the knowledge it took them decades to attain. If you're brand new to this hobby, the best thing you can do is to pay close attention to those who look like professionals. Listen to what they say, and discretely watch what they do on the beach. Notice where they hunt, when they hunt, and where they walk. You will ultimately see patterns that offer clues to their success.

The second thing you can do is to join every seashell, fossil, and shark tooth hunting forum you can find. This will allow you to gather pertinent information from the pros without having to be so much of a creeper on the beach. While many of these experts don't intend to give away their secrets, you can extract a mountain of details from reading their posts, analyzing their pictures, and then integrating those details into your own strategy. A later chapter about resources lists the best forums to follow daily to learn more from the heavyweights at the pinnacle of their game.

These first two things should really just be a springboard into your individual shelling journey, however. The very best part of this hobby is exploring and finding new experiences for yourself. Combine what you learn from this book and from other sources, but set out on your own path because every beach is worth a look. The longtime shellers have found the right beaches for them—now you need to find the right beaches for you. Don't feel pressured to go where everybody else is hunting—no one likes overcrowded and overhunted beaches. Instead, use your free time to actually be free. While your experimentation with new places will result in hits and misses, you'll never regret the adventure.

When asked about the best way for new shellers to accelerate their learning, a very successful sheller once replied, "Put yourself on as many beaches as you can as often as you can, and walk as far as your legs will carry you." There will be a lot of trial and error in your early years. Even most experts will admit that they're still tinkering around with their strategy and coming to new realizations all the time. The value of the exploration is realized once you start finding unexpected things on your extended walkabouts. Pictured above is the ram's horn shell. It's the internal shell of a tiny squid, and they're usually tucked in the dry seaweed at the high wrack line. If you want one, focus on hunting the beaches on the Atlantic side of the Florida Keys.

Shelling Strategy

Plotting Your Moves in Advance

The great twentieth-century writer Ernest Hemingway once wrote in an article that "you must be prepared to work always without applause." This perspective offers a useful parallel to shelling because of both the amount of dedication it takes to succeed and the reality that the effort doesn't always pan out. One thing is for sure, though: the skilled shellers who are going on a hunt tomorrow are investing time in thinking about their strategy today. You might be asking yourself, "What is there to think about? Don't you just walk out onto the nearest beach and start hunting?" Certainly plenty of shellers do that. You can stumble out onto any stretch of coastline and get going whenever you please. But you wouldn't have this book in your hand if you didn't want to know how to improve your game plan. The following chapters unveil the behind-the-scenes thought processes that guide the steps of the world's most successful beachcombers. The people in this community are in a constant state of calculating and observing to make the best choices for the next day's hunt. The upcoming chapters reveal the variables that influence the calculus that the analytical shellers are constantly working in their brains. This is the part they never say out loud, so get ready to take notes.

The prospect of what might wind up in the next day's shelling bucket is enough to keep any sheller awake the night before.

Identifying Shell Beds and Wrack Lines

As a shell hunter, you want to be where the largest concentration of shells is available. They get deposited in a strip called a wrack line—a narrow band of organic material usually at the highest point the tide reached that day. You can often look up the beach and see remnants of wrack lines from higher storm tides in the past. Additional smaller wrack lines can also form lower on the beach. On a day when you have a lot of company out there by the ocean's edge, you want to be hunting the freshest wrack line (the one that was most recently covered with water). Wrack lines run parallel to the ocean, and they will be in a relatively straight line as you walk down the beach. A shell bed is a deposit of seashells and fossils left behind in clumps on the beach after a tide recedes. Because of this, they usually occur sporadically and wash down perpendicular to the ocean. Also called shell hash, these piles of material can be found anywhere, and on a really good day the whole beach will be covered with them. Shell beds and wrack lines are the places to look for the best volume of seashells and shark teeth, especially when the tide is washing over them.

Sanibel Island, Florida, is renowned for its colorful shell hash. All of the pinks, oranges, and yellows glisten like hard candy. Once you've seen it in person, you'll compare all other beaches to it, and most will fall woefully short in comparison.

Most wrack lines high on the beach contain leaves and seaweed. Sneaky things get caught up there too, so even though it may look like just a pile of garbage, always scan it.

The first thing veteran hunters do when they get out on a beach is inspect the shell beds to see what information can be gleaned. For instance, if the shell hash has bigger pieces and some whole shells, that's a good indicator that it's going to be a successful day. Fine, broken-up hash material usually indicates that smaller seashells and shark teeth are more likely in those areas. Many hunters can also study these shell piles to figure out which species are washing out and thus what else might be available that day. One way to do that is by identifying the species in the fossil context and making inferences about what else might be connected to it in the same geologic period. The color, appearance, and content of shell hash vary at each beach you visit. Sometimes the hash is rocky and mostly brown or black. Other locations have beaches covered with white coral rocks and little bursts of colorful shells in the mix. Even

Sometimes the ocean will deposit a wrack line that includes both debris and shells. Notice here that the lightweight plant material was pushed high and the heavier shell hash pulled low.

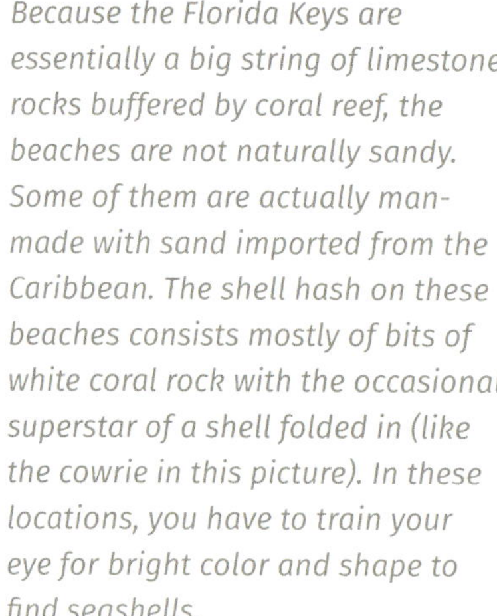

Because the Florida Keys are essentially a big string of limestone rocks buffered by coral reef, the beaches are not naturally sandy. Some of them are actually man-made with sand imported from the Caribbean. The shell hash on these beaches consists mostly of bits of white coral rock with the occasional superstar of a shell folded in (like the cowrie in this picture). In these locations, you have to train your eye for bright color and shape to find seashells.

Note the difference between Florida Keys shell hash in the previous picture and Topsail Island, North Carolina, shell hash pictured here. There are phenomenal things to find in both locations. You'll just have to adjust your vision to hunt in very different beach contexts. Also, I hope your eye was drawn to the white shell in the middle of this photo. It's a yummy little Scotch bonnet.

beaches that are just a few miles apart can have dramatically different shell hash.

The visual tendency of most beachcombers is to focus *in the middle* of the biggest shell bed. Very often there's a lot to be found on the periphery or in the shell beds that are slightly smaller. Be sure to move your eyes to the edges of the shell beds (particularly at the top). The heavier material tends to get washed up at the top of the bed, and then because of its weight it stays put. You'll often notice that the smaller grainy material gets pulled down low. Don't expend very much time looking in shell beds that have been raked with a tool by a previous beachcomber because that altered landscape interferes with your ability to see. Shells that were washed off by the receding tide are clean and easy to see; raking puts sand back on them and makes it harder for shellers who come behind.

Hunky, chunky shell hash is what you want to see when you step out on the beach in the morning. This is the kind of shell bed where the pros will make several stealth passes without calling attention to the heightened potential of the area.

Reading the Tide Charts

The most important thing to do in preparation for any beach hunt is to consult a free online tide chart. You can find them with a simple internet search like "Carmel Beach, California, tide chart April 2025." Look at the day on the calendar when you're going to the beach to get two critical pieces of information: the times on the clock when the tides will be high and low and what height they will be (measured in feet) at those times. While many online organizations provide free tide charts, Tidetime.org offers the most readable information.

The height measurement of a tide does not reflect the number of feet up on the beach the water will go horizontally. Instead, it's a vertical measure of how many feet above or below the average water level (indicated by zero on the tide chart) the ocean will rise or fall. This zero mark is also sometimes referred to as the tide chart datum.

Tide charts are location specific, and even beaches that are in very close proximity to each other can have slightly different tidal patterns. Be sure you are consulting the tide chart that applies to the beach you'll be hunting.

To understand why data about wave height and tidal frequency are so vital to the success of your trip, you have to learn a bit about how the tides operate.

Most coastal locations on Earth have two high tides and two low tides. The tides run in a cycle of twenty-four hours and fifty minutes: high, low, high, low each day. Every transition from one tide to the next takes six hours and a few minutes, so the morning high tide tomorrow is going to be later than the morning high tide was today. There are exceptions when a beach will not have two high tides and two low tides in a day, however. As well, you'll sometimes see on a tide chart that the difference in feet from a high tide to a low tide is not a wide range, meaning the tide line is not going to move dramatically that day. Those circumstances are usually not ideal for shelling because the movement of the water is what keeps things stirred up in the shell hash.

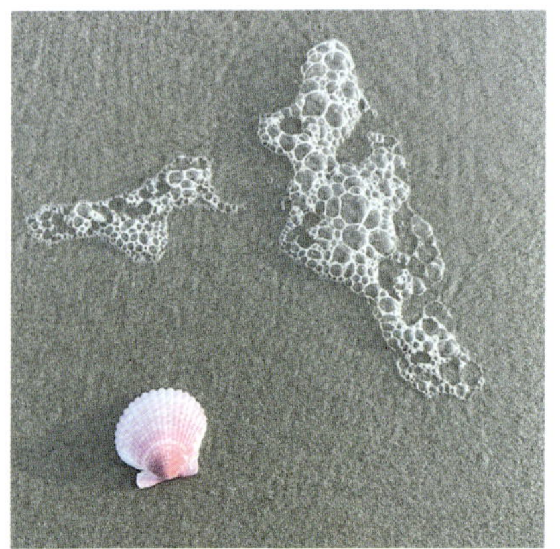

The height of the tide in feet matters because you have to know where the water is going to be at all times in relation to the shell beds on the beach. Very often, participants in seashell forums dispense horrible advice when a newcomer seeks advice: "I'm going to Padre Island, Texas, tomorrow. When is the best time to get the premium shells?" Inevitably, someone will chime in

It could be argued that a working knowledge of the tidal patterns is the single most important strategic factor that distinguishes the successful shell hunters from those who are still working to reach their full potential. Unlocking the power of the tides can result in a bucketful of top-shelf shells like those pictured above. These jewels were found on a single morning walk in the Ten Thousand Islands in Florida.

with the stock answer: "Two hours before low tide." That response is such a rigid way to think about the factors that influence shell activity, and this advice is responsible for so many people leaving the beach disappointed.

As we learned in the previous chapter, you want to be on the beach when the water is actively washing over the shell beds. Tide chart information should be used to put you on the beach during the precise time that's happening. If the advantageous shell beds have materialized low on the beach landscape, the standard "two hours before low tide" response works beautifully. However, if the shell beds happen to reveal themselves at the high line and you show up to hunt two hours before low tide, you're going to be three hours too late. By then the expert shellers who read the tide more accurately will be back at home rinsing the bucket of marvelous shells they collected while you waited.

To maximize the chances of finding the best shells (like this utterly perfect lion's paw), you want your eyes to see the shell beds first on an outgoing tide. This requires knowledge of the exact times of the high and low tides.

The receding tide (when the water begins to go out from its highest mark) is the most advantageous time to hunt for seashells. To know when that is, you have to consult the tide chart daily. Because the receding tide provides such opportunity, consider hunting for the entire six hours that the water is falling high to low. If it becomes apparent that no shell beds are emerging lower on the beach, you may cut your stay short and not hunt for the entire tide.

One of the main benefits of becoming experienced at hunting the same beach location is that you'll learn to look at a tide chart and know whether the water will make any dramatic moves that might result in better beachcombing. By recognizing the average high-tide mark in feet of your favorite beach, any outlier tides that go way above that will catch your eye in the charting. If there's a consistent line of shells at that high wrack line, you need to arrive an hour before the high tide to watch the water rush over those shells and then begin to recede. That first hour of hunting might not be spectacular. You'll probably have much better results when the waves begin to pull back at the peak of the high tide because that downward thrust of the water makes new seashells and fossils show themselves. Your goal is to be there at the precise moment the tide shifts because things can change for the better in an instant.

Perhaps the best way to demonstrate how to build a tidal strategy is through a specific example. On a recent trip to Holden Beach, North Carolina, I was working with the daily tide chart listed below.

High tide 2:09 a.m. 4.03 feet
Low tide 8:43 a.m. 0.60 feet
High tide 2:31 p.m. 3.20 feet
Low tide 8:47 p.m. 0.44 feet

I knew from the previous day that the beach had only one predominant wrack of shells, and it was a relatively high line that didn't get pulled down with the falling tide. (While the beach does change every day, you can garner all kinds of information on the previous day that will help you identify potential patterns for the next day.) Because of my knowledge of that high wrack line, I looked at the tide chart and knew I should arrive at the beach around 1:00 in the morning and stay until around 4:00 a.m. Once the water stopped washing over the beds, the hunt completely dried up within the span of about an hour. The people who waited until two hours before low tide and arrived around 6:45 a.m. left empty-handed because they missed the window. As well, think of how many shellers would just see 6:45 a.m. on the clock and think of it as the time to go "early shelling." On this tidal cycle, their idea of early was actually way too late. Learning to read the tides for your beach is the key to identifying when those brief windows of superb shelling might occur each day.

It's also important to note that on this day with the shells where they were, I didn't even bother going back to the beach for the second high tide at 2:31 p.m. It only reached 3.20 feet, which I knew wasn't high enough for the water to rush over that blockbuster high shell line. Peak shelling requires that the ocean either reveal a new shell bed or wash over an existing one. There probably wasn't going to be anything new to see until the next highest tide the following morning. Being able to apply this kind of predictive knowledge will save you so much time, energy, and gas money.

Conversely, it's important to be cognizant of the average low tide mark in feet, particularly if you frequent a beach where a lot of quality material floats around at the low line. On a beach like that, an altered strategy would have been necessary based on the information gathered from the tide chart. With no shells high on the beach, it would have been advantageous to wait until

Having long-term familiarity with a beach location will help you understand the nuances of the tides that can give you a shelling advantage. For instance, in the Florida Keys, you don't always notice an immediate reduction in the depth of the water as a tide begins to fall. Because it can sometimes take a few hours for that water to start receding with the lowered tide, you should factor that location-specific data into your plan, especially if you would like to rent a boat to go shelling at a time when the tide is just right.

the second low tide of the day at 8:47 p.m. because it dipped lower by 0.16 feet than the first low tide. That would have allowed for more time to hunt material on the beach that was still covered by water with the earlier low tide. In this situation, plotting an arrival time of 6:45 p.m. would be the best strategy. If you're hunting in southwest Florida, the lower tide is often the best time to be out. Especially if you're dealing with tidal pools or very still clear water in the lower part of a tide, you'll notice the minute the tide shifts in the other direction and starts coming in again. There will be more ripples in the water that take away the visibility you were probably enjoying.

What all of this means is that familiarity with the beach where you hunt is critically important and consulting the tide chart daily is absolutely vital if you want to do well. Most shellers are unaware of this, but experienced

The benefit of learning to read the tides is manifested not just in volume but in variety. The menagerie of desirable shells pictured above from Marco Island, Florida, was gathered on a favorable early morning tide that peaked at a really low mark about two hours before most shellers got onto the beach for their morning walks. The potential of the tide (with both the number of feet it was going to go below the zero mark and the timing, which effectively reduced competition) was evident simply in the information gathered from a quick look at a tide chart.

Even when top-tier shellers are in the vicinity of a beach they really love to hunt, they often won't go if the tide chart info isn't encouraging. Shelling is a physically demanding hobby, so you have to be smart about how you expend your energy.

beachcombers actually look at the tide charts months and sometimes up to a year in advance so they can schedule their lodging and transportation for vacations during favorable tides. Many of the ferries that take shellers to really productive shelling grounds book up months in advance of promising tides because the hardcore shellers always have their eyes on the charts.

While you're studying your tide chart, you also need to pay close attention to the moon phases, as the moon controls the tides. We'll take a deep dive into that in the next chapter and learn about special circumstances related to the moon that cause the tides to go very high and very low.

Picking the Best Moon

Even though there aren't very many expert shellers talking about it, it's widely known that the full moon is the best time for beachcombing. The next best moon phase is the new moon, but it's really a distant runner-up. The gravitational force of the moon controls the tidal patterns on Earth. However, when Earth, the moon, and the sun align, the sun's effect on the tides joins the party, creating an intense push and pull that will make the tide go super high on the beach and then extra low. When the tide goes high—sometimes several feet or more higher than the average high tide—and then goes wildly low, it's called a spring tide or a king tide.

That extreme low tide can be the key that unlocks everything for a sheller in a place like the Ten Thousand Islands of Florida. When these ultra-low tides go below the zero mark in feet on the tide chart, the numbers get into negative territory. This is called a negative low tide. A negative low tide is denoted on tide charts with a negative sign in front of the feet in the low tide column. The larger the negative number, the farther out the water will go. In areas where the water is already fairly shallow like Marco Island or Keewaydin Island, a negative low tide will allow the sheller to walk way out onto sand that's almost always covered by ocean. Treasures that have been covered up sometimes for almost a year will be exposed on that negative low.

You can predict when these favorable negative low tides will happen by

It's necessary to look way ahead in the tide charts to know when the spring or king tides are coming because they happen only a few times each year. But when you hit them right, they produce the most incredible results. You can read the tide charts for any beach location up to a year in advance to craft your plan for catching the most favorable conditions. The expert shellers are planning this far ahead on the calendar and booking their boat tickets and hotel rooms. You can't beat them unless you join them.

surveying the charts months in advance. Let's examine a sample Marco Island, Florida, tide chart on a full moon to learn how to read it.

Low tide 6:21 a.m. –0.75 feet
High tide 1:17 p.m. 2.33 feet
Low tide 6:05 p.m. 1.28 feet
High tide 11:55 p.m. 3.07 feet

The first thing you should notice is the negative sign in front of the tide height on the first low tide of the day at 6:21 a.m. That is very low water for Marco Island. On that particular tide, the serious hunters would begin around 3:30 a.m. and scour the beach until the water stops dropping just after 6:00 a.m. Again, for most new beachcombers just getting started with the hobby, they would probably think 6:30 in the morning would make them an early bird, but on this tide they would be painfully tardy. The second noteworthy detail on this tide chart is the second high tide at 11:55 p.m. That 3.07 feet indicator shows you the highest the water will be on the beach that day. That 11:55 p.m. tide mark could have a lot of potential for a high line of shells.

The negative low tides don't just happen randomly, with the water going back to more average ranges the next day. As the calendar days pass leading up to and following a full moon, you'll see the numbers on the low tides start to gradually get lower, heading toward the favorable moon and then gradually getting higher as you move away from the day with the full moon. Sometimes you'll get five or six days in a row with good negative lows, and that's when you want to book your vacation. With some practice you can learn to analyze the water levels in this way, giving you an edge over other beachcombers who are just randomly picking days to hunt. If you're diligent about studying the charts and gain the ability to recognize the tidal activity that influences the shelling on your favorite beach, each year there will be four or five weeks that jump out at you as golden opportunities.

When we get to the first and last quarter phases of the moon, the pull of the tide gets weaker. This is called a neap tide, and during this phase the differences in feet between the high and low will diminish. In general, the quarter phases of the moon aren't the best time to hunt. Neap tides are an excellent time to catch up on your sleep.

Charting Wind Directions

One of the least considered factors in the shelling equation is wind speed and direction, mainly because not very many people think about their potential influence and the winds can be an intricate puzzle. Sure, the conventional wisdom suggests that big wind events like hurricanes and tropical storms tend to produce better shelling. Very few people, on the other hand, factor in the influence of everyday winds and how they might impact what washes up on the beach. To reach the pinnacle of this hobby, you have to take dozens of factors into account each day, with the wind often overlooked.

The first thing to know about wind direction is that its repercussions are going to be different for every beach that you search. In the case of Sanibel Island, Florida, where each year tens of thousands of shellers try to crack the island's code, there have been those who have made a life of studying the winds. Some of these experts have been able to determine which wind directions are best for *specific beaches*, and the island itself is only twelve miles long. Sanibel is unique because it sits sideways in the ocean (perpendicular to Florida's peninsula). Because of that geographical position, the shells just roll up into it when the winds are right. Though you do see some disagreement among Sanibel locals on this issue, there is definite consensus around north, west, and northwest winds being the best. The experts on the island recommend the west and northwest winds particularly. At Holden Beach in North Carolina, south, west, and southwest winds are optimal.

It's a mighty good feeling to walk out on the beach in the morning and see the shell beds popped out after a night of winds whose favorability you predicted.

This is what it looks like when I have the beach to myself in the middle of the night and the winds are right. When the winds whip up in southwest Florida, the alphabet cones start rolling. Their spellbinding color patterns make them obvious, which is why you want to catch the tide at the right time to be there when they first make their appearance.

The geographical position of the different beaches you visit will require you to chart wind directions over time to develop the formula for your favorite areas. What works for Port Aransas, Texas, may not work for South Padre Island to the south because that stretch of coastline bends. The analysis required to figure out these tricky elements of the ocean's behavior can take years to sort out, and for those who are naturally curious and drawn to competitive activities, it's the best kind of nerdy fun to work on these long-term projects and try to be the first to determine the right answer.

To avoid speaking in absolutes here, note that there are exceptions when the "favorable" factors we have discussed don't actually play out as anticipated. For instance, a really strong wind blowing in the wrong direction can thwart the impact of a full moon or a new moon whose tides looked great on paper. More often than not, though, considering the factors outlined in this section in your planning process will lead to your best opportunity for success.

Capitalizing on Fall Storms and Strong Winter Currents

It's no secret that fall tropical storms and hurricanes can result in huge washouts of amazing seashells and fossils. Nearly every "Top 10 Tips for Shelling" list encourages hunting after a storm. A dear friend in the National Guard was once deployed to a North Carolina beach community after Hurricane Fran in 1996, and as one of the first people on the ground afterward, he saw massive whole seashells washed across the road from the ocean and into the yards of the second row of houses. Clearly if everyday winds impact the shelling equation, massive winds can have exponential effects.

There's a great deal of nuance that goes along with those strong winds, though, and not very many people contemplate those particulars. To exploit the beachcombing potential of a storm, you'll need to use what you know about the directional impact of the wind on the particular beach you'll hunt. The wind direction matters so much because if it's blowing wrong at seventy-five or a hundred miles per hour, the storm is going to suck everything down off the beach or push sand onto the beach. After the remnants of Hurricane Ian came through in 2022, friends who were hunting in Myrtle Beach and Cherry Grove in South Carolina and Ocean Isle in North Carolina all said the hurricane had pulled every bit of material off the beach. There wasn't even a broken seashell to be found. Just slightly north in Holden Beach, more at the top of the ark that the coastline makes leading up to Bald Head Island, North Carolina, the post-hurricane shelling was off the charts. As hurricanes and tropical storms pass over, the directions of

the winds shift, so whatever direction the wind was blowing when the storm exited Holden Beach was ideal.

The general consensus among shellers is that any wind over twenty miles per hour can have a significant effect on the beachcombing potential. Sustained winds of thirty-nine miles per hour indicate a low-level tropical storm. Therefore, you don't necessarily need a named system to make a difference in your shelling. This is why perennial beachcombers monitor the extended weather forecasts to the point of obsession.

As tempted as you might be, you do have to wait for the storm to pass before you go out there. And this tip might give you a bit more patience as you wait: a storm's impact isn't always felt immediately afterward. Very often the shelling doesn't crescendo until *twenty-four or forty-eight hours after the storm is gone*. The reason is that the enticing shells that may have been dislodged by favorable winds can't make it to shore until the wave heights recede. Sometimes Mother Ocean just needs a few tides to get herself back in order. So if you go to the beach with high hopes after a storm, be disciplined and wait through a few tides.

One of the drawbacks of an ocean churned up by the winds is the amount of sea foam that might wash in after a storm. It's nasty, and it can completely mask the shell beds.

Notice how the sea foam covering the lower half of this shell bed obscures your vision.

Even six months after Hurricane Ian, hazardous debris was still washing onto the beach. In unique hunting situations like this, it's vital that you keep your shoes on and select footwear with hard rubber soles. Rusty nails would cut right through the bottom of most water shoes, and nobody wants a tetanus shot on vacation.

Be sure to test your jackets, coats, and hats to see that they're effective at blocking wind before you go out into the field. Also, read the tags so you know what kind of gear you're buying. If you get "windproof" fabrics, that basically means you'll still be cold from the wind, but you'll survive. "Wind resistant" means that the jacket will do nothing, and you don't stand a chance. As well, you'll be glad that you applied extra facial moisturizer and lip balm before heading out on particularly windy days. Wind burns can feel worse than sun burns.

Importantly, the dangers associated with storm hunting should not be underestimated. You can't drive into an area where there are active storm watches, warnings, and curfews. If something happens to you, rescue personnel are going to have to put themselves at risk to help you, diverting attention away from others who may need assistance more. Getting to the beach after a storm can put you in the middle of rising water across roadways, on top of fallen power lines, and under trees and limbs that are in danger of falling. Debris on the beach and in the water, including nails, rusty metal, and broken glass, can also be incredibly hazardous. Boards from piers, decks, and walkways are often rolling around in the waves immediately following hurricanes. Those who got to see southwest Florida after Hurricane Ian remember numerous household appliances floating in the waves.

While you're keeping track of wind directions and their influence on shelling for your most loved beaches, add in the data from post-storm days. Note the direction the winds are blowing *at the end of the weather event* by using a service like Windy.com. The satisfaction of cracking the wind code is real, my friends, so don't delay in buying a notebook to use as a beachcombing log.

Recognizing the Advantage of Unpleasant Weather

It sounds absurd, but many hardcore shellers look for bad weather in the forecast to plot opportunity. They intentionally plan beach trips when they see that the conditions might deter others. With fewer people looking, a bigger percentage of the loot will go in your treasure chest. All it takes is a tiny sprinkle of rain to weed out the fair-weather hunters. Those remaining are likely the ones whose shell haul pictures you admire. They succeeded by walking for six hours in the cold rain. Scope out your local forecast to see when cold temperatures, rain (with no lightning chance), or wind might keep other people away. It's exceedingly rare on the beaches in the Southeast, but hunting in the sleet or snow usually means you'll be on your own. No weather forecasting technology is going to get it right all the time, but AccuWeather tends to be fairly reliable and can be accessed for free online.

If you're traveling, be sure to pack the gear you'll need to hunt in all kinds of conditions no matter the forecast. There are many companies producing very compact and effective foul-weather jackets and suits that fold up easily and are lightweight for transport. You won't be able to hang for very long in cold and/or wet conditions if you're miserable, so investing in the right gear will serve you well for a long time.

It's always a winner when a quick rain shower clears the lightweights off the beach. Anyway, it's probably best that they're in their hotels and cars not getting their hair wet. Rainy days also provide unparalleled opportunities to spot wildlife. Luckily, they aren't so concerned about their hair.

This was a "RealFeel" thirteen-degree day—not an environment suitable for whiners and complainers. You've got to want it bad to endure cold like that, and you're going to need one of those Arctic explorer coats with a faux fur hood to survive it.

Studying Shells as Hunting Preparation

One of the best ways to prepare yourself to find great seashells is to study examples of the species that are still on your bucket list. Looking at pictures (like the ones in this book) is a wonderful start, but it's highly recommended that you buy examples of the species you've never found so you can inspect them in person. This examination will allow you to recognize the distinguishing features, shapes, patterns, colors, and textures of your most desired species so that if you're on a beach where the opportunity arises, your eyes will be ready. By studying the specifics of that shell, you'll finally be able to recognize it on your own in the field.

Focus on purchasing species that are native to the places that you actually hunt. Most of the seashell shops are filled with imports, species you're likely never to encounter on a U.S. beach. As well, many of the shells sourced internationally are taken from the sea with the live creatures still in them. They're harvested specifically for the sale of the shell and not to consume

She Sells Sea Shells on Periwinkle Way in Sanibel, Florida, is an excellent place to buy examples of the desirable native species of southwest Florida to study at home. And while you're there, don't forget to have your picture taken in front of the junonia mailbox.

the animal for sustenance. We don't want to support a rotten global trade like that. When you're buying seashells, always ask where they came from (vendors rarely know), and support the shops that are sourcing local shells gathered by ethical beachcombers.

The Scotch bonnet is an excellent candidate for purchasing and studying. Their lighter colors tend to make them blend in with the rest of the shell hash on the beach. The value in owning one is that you can train your eyes to see the subtle characteristics that allow you to distinguish it among the other shells.

OPPOSITE: *Spend as much time as possible holding and looking at the varieties of seashells you want to find on your own. Get your eyes used to the wrinkly knobs of the Caribbean vase shell and the way the brown periostracum coating contrasts with the white of the shell shining through.*

Researching and Troubleshooting

The most accomplished shellers are the ones who approach their pursuit as a lifelong learning hobby. As such, they research and read constantly. They use what they see and learn each day as recognizance for plotting their location and strategy for the future. When this information reveals that their plan might need to be adjusted, they're flexible enough to change course.

This kind of troubleshooting takes a lot of time, but you'll see how quickly your knowledge base grows because of the dedicated effort. As you follow shelling and fossil experts online and participate in the forums, be sure to use the search bar before you ask a question. You don't want to be responsible for repeating content with a query that has already been asked fifty times. While most proficient shellers are welcoming to those who have questions, there is the expectation that you'll eventually fly on your own and need support only when you find something really unusual. In a recent shell forum, the original poster mentioned evidence of a red tide at a beach, and someone asked, "What is red tide?" It's a reasonable question—but one that should have been answered with a Google search. Ask only when you genuinely don't know and you have already put in a little bit of effort to find the answer on your own.

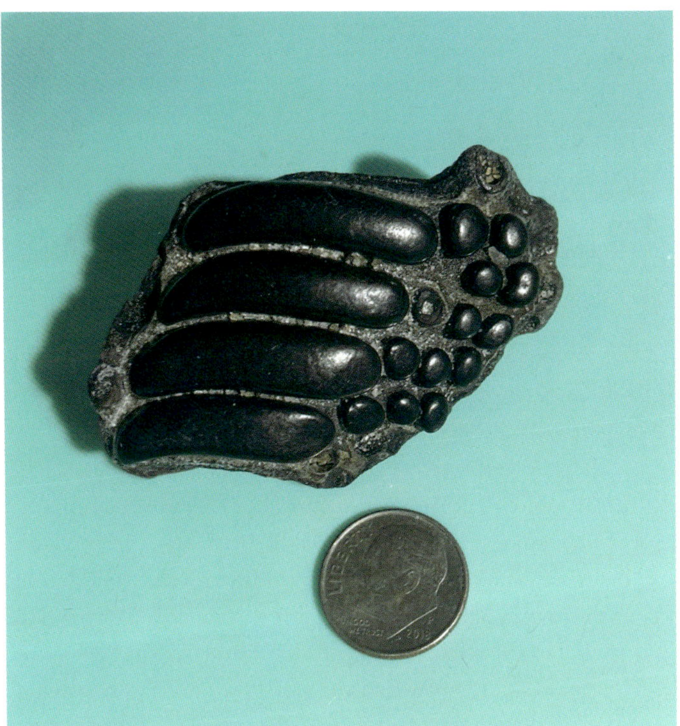

The first time I found one, I was totally stumped. Fortunately, I had a friend who quickly identified it as a fossilized fish mouth plate via text. Have you ever seen anything so cool?

From the pool of more skilled people you meet, you should try to assemble a posse of shell hunters. Text them when you're on a local beach that's hitting that day. Give them the inside scoop, and they'll likely do the same for you. And if you visit a beach that turns out to be disappointing one day, give them a heads-up so they don't make the trip. Tell them where the shell beds are so they can choose the right time in the tide. It's best to keep your tribe very small. If your community gets too big, it can be exhausting keeping up with the communication each day.

As you delve more deeply into this hobby, you'll need people around you to help identify really strange and rare things you find. It's nice to be able to do that with a text and get a fast answer. Once you know enough to help others learn, be sure to give more than you take from these exchanges.

Tracking Beach Renourishment Projects

Beach renourishment is the importation of new sand (either through transplanting it with dump trucks or pumping it from offshore) to repair a beach that's suffering from erosion. Also called nourishment, replenishment, or dredging, these projects are often contracted at the cost of millions of dollars after a beach community has experienced either short-term erosion from a tropical storm or hurricane or long-term erosion from the everyday encroachment of the ocean. Some communities are on a regular schedule of renourishment because their beaches are so sensitive.

Many environmentalists and government officials suggest that these refurbishments are eco-friendly. Even a little bit of common sense reveals the red flags associated with that logic. Running gargantuan earth-moving

All you have to say to Carolina beachcombers is "Holden" and they know exactly what you mean. Holden Beach, North Carolina, officials renourished the beach in 2022. The machines hit a layer of Cretaceous material that sent collectors into a frenzy. In addition to incredible fossils like the ones pictured above, lion's paws, flat scallops, Scotch bonnets, junonias, and giant Atlantic murexes were washing out. Holden's renourishment also benefited shellers for a lot longer than most projects do. The beach was still producing even two years afterward, which is highly unusual. Once initial word spread about what was happening, people from all over the country flocked to "Golden Holden" to see what the fuss was about. All of the teeth in this image were found over the course of two days.

machines on a beach is bad news. Dumping tons of sand into a functioning food chain disrupts everything. Tiny animals are smothered. Species that might want to roost or nest on those beaches are completely freaked out. Every part of the ecosystem is affected, all the way down to water quality.

Mother Ocean will take what she wants, and it's never a good idea for humans to try to change her plans. It was, after all, our own stupidity for building structures so close to a moving ocean.

With all that said, beach renourishment can create the perfect environment for shellers to hit paydirt, especially if the project involves pumping sand from offshore and operators running the machines at a speed that allows the big shells and large fossils to make it to the beach. When the operation involves pumping, you can see the offshore barges, which are connected to colossal tubes that run to the shore. During this time, the beach is almost always closed to pedestrians while the bulldozers move the sand around to flatten out the surface. Sometimes these replenishments do nothing but sling blank sand onto the beach. If the pumps don't hit a quality vein of material or if the technicians run the pumps at a speed that prevents larger material from passing through, the renourishment could actually ruin what was a fertile shelling beach. If, however, the pumps strike gold, some of the finest shelling activity you've ever seen might unfold, especially if you're first when the beach reopens. That's why so many people stalk the municipal websites in their area to track when beach renourishment projects are scheduled and when specific beaches will be opening afterward.

Because of the force the machines use to move the sand and the fact that earthmovers drive over the sand afterward, a lot of the new material that gets deposited is damaged. It's very common to find broken megalodon teeth after replenished beaches reopen. Fossils and seashells oftentimes don't fare well in the process, but some of them sneak through unscathed, and that's why the really serious folks in the hunting community constantly monitor the progress of these projects.

The bump from these renourishments is usually short-lived (a year or less), but while it's happening, you can end up finding incredible quality and mind-blowing quantity.

Choosing Your Location

Every beach changes with every tide. Some hunts will result in a bounty, and the very next tide on the same day can be a bust. While there are some beaches that are naturally better than others for shelling, nobody can offer guarantees about any location. There'll be plenty of days when even the beaches on this very selective list are not producing.

As in real estate, location is everything. If you choose the wrong beach, none of the other strategies in this book will matter because there may literally be nothing to find on that beach other than sand. This rough overview of locations in the United States will highlight the places that are *usually good*. The beaches showcased here are where the shelling hotbeds often

are—therefore, these are the places where experienced shellers book their vacations and where they pull off the interstate for a pit stop if they're traveling somewhere else. Essentially, you can find shells on any beach across coastal America, whether you're talking about the Northeast or the Pacific Northwest. The goal with this text is to put you on top of the most remarkable shells in the largest quantity and to give you some basic logistical tips to help with navigating these beach communities. You'll notice the curated choices here are heavy on Florida and the Carolinas. That's not a sign of bias—those areas just seem to be where Mother Ocean likes to do her best work. We'll skip over many outstanding shelling beaches because there are just too many to name individually. We don't have space here to discuss every notable stop along the way, so if your favorite strip of sand got left off the list, please don't get a shell in your shoe.

Public service announcement: Once you arrive at the idyllic locations that are about to be revealed, please refrain from talking on speakerphone out there. Even the birds don't like it, and they're usually pretty easygoing.

Outer Banks of North Carolina

The Outer Banks of North Carolina is a chain of islands that stretches for nearly two hundred miles, so you won't find a pinpoint location for them on the map. What you will find is seashells—incomprehensible seashells. Now not every beach in that two-hundred-mile stretch is going to yield results, and you may need to take a shelling charter or ferry to get out to a productive island, but if you work it just right, you won't soon forget the experience. The Outer Banks offer a sheller's bonanza, particularly for species that are difficult to find in other places, like Scotch bonnets, helmet shells, and tuns. While some of the barrier islands are known to be top-ten shelling locations in America, the next island down might be a big, fat zero for beachcombing. Some of the locations that get a lot of attention for being consistently good are Shackleford Banks, Hatteras (specifically Frisco Beach), Ocracoke, Cape Lookout, Buxton, Pea Island, and Portsmouth Island. Many of these places are accessible only by ferry, charter, or private boat, so a lot of advanced planning is needed. If you're thinking about booking a trip, you should spend a few weeks searching "Outer Banks" in the online shelling forums to see recent pictures of beachcombers with their finds. It's also worth following charter boat companies on social media because they post what their clients are finding almost daily. That research can give you a sense of precisely where you need to be around the time that you're thinking about traveling. While in the Outer Banks, don't expect to find shark teeth. Many visitors are puzzled by that because the rest of the Carolinas have such an amazing fossil record. It's just a dead zone for teeth, but there are enough seashells to keep you busy.

The Shackleford Island ferry runs out of Beaufort, North Carolina, and it's a very affordable way to see the southern edge of the Outer Banks. You might even spot some wild horses while you're on the island. If you are so lucky, remember you have to keep a considerable distance, especially if you observe horses with foals. The ferry ride takes about twenty minutes. Advance reservations are recommended.

One of the secrets to hunting well in the Outer Banks is paying attention to the very high wrack line (up in the dry sand). The middle part of the beach may not give up much, but the high line is almost always packed with prizes. Visiting these islands on a negative low tide will also reveal buckets of shells that can't be left behind. Be prepared to get in the water to find them, and be mindful of the strong currents (especially at the tips of islands, like the point on Shackleford Banks where the ferry passengers disembark).

Lastly, many of the islands in the Outer Banks are considered protected National Seashores and are thus managed by the National Park Service, with specific guidelines about what you can and can't remove from the beach. Make sure you know the rules that pertain to your hunting location.

Many of the islands in the Outer Banks have wild landscapes, rough surf, and unpredictable weather. Beachcombers who hunt there should be prepared to walk long distances on beaches without facilities.

One of the most staggering things for virgin visitors to the Outer Banks is the number of enormous helmets that often dot the shoreline. It's not uncommon to scoop up ten of them in just a few hours. Mesh bags with shoulder straps, which many shellers use for beachcombing, are not sufficient for the number and size of helmets you'll find in this area. Buckets are a must, and if you're toying with the idea of taking a long walk, a beach wagon will be your best buddy out there.

Onslow Beach, North Carolina

Onslow Beach is legendary for shelling and fossil hunting. There's just one catch, though: the beach is located on the Camp Lejeune Marine Corps base, and you must have military credentials to access it. Anyone with valid clearance and a Department of Defense identification card can pass through the gates and can bring visitors as long as they all fit in one car. Before you go out, be sure to check if any part of the beach is closed for temporary military maneuvers. One of the reasons Onslow is so fantastic is because even on a busy day there are very few people there. Once you head out and are facing the ocean, walk to the right because beach access is always restricted less than a mile away in the other direction. If you go too far, a foreboding voice on a military bullhorn will blare at you from a tower, and you'll likely drop your shell bucket. By heading to the right, you can walk for about four miles until you get to the point at the New River Inlet, and the entire walk is exquisite. Onslow is famous for its big shark teeth (including regular megalodon finds in really surprising colors). The beach also offers up flat scallops, lion's paws, horse conchs, and all kinds of other riches. Because it's a military base, there are also bullet casings laying around from decades of training exercises. It's common to discover casings ranging from the 1970s to the 1990s on the surface with no metal detecting required. If you have a way to get out to Onslow, avail yourself of it without delay.

Having shell envy isn't a good look. However, it's hard not to with this tun shell found by my shelltastic friend Rene Vance at Onslow Beach.

Onslow is such an unpredictable place because the shell hash often looks routine and boring. Just when you least expect it, something fabulous reveals itself, like this glorious merlot-colored scallop with a dainty white edge.

Those who have never been to Onslow are desperate to find a way out there. Those who know of its richness are constantly daydreaming about going back.

Topsail Island, North Carolina

Don't be dismayed if you can't gain access to Onslow Beach because Topsail Island is the next one down in North Carolina, and it's a total delight. Topsail is a huge island—stretching twenty-six miles top to bottom—so with that many beach access points, the crowd really spreads out. You'll never feel cramped. The first and second access points after coming into North Topsail and taking a left onto New River Inlet Road usually have a good amount of parking. Among the people who shell there frequently, there's great debate about whether North or South Topsail is better. Insanely big shark teeth are regularly found on both, and the people who live on the island have amassed awe-inspiring shell collections over the years by regularly walking the shoreline. The shells gathered there are the premium species that everyone wants. Topsail is also a fairly easy stopping point for a quick detour if you're traveling somewhere else via Highway 17.

Only good things can come from walking through these gates.

It's a rare thing to walk off a beach with lion's paws, flat scallops, and mermaid's purses in hand after just a short stroll, but Topsail Island can deliver such a menagerie.

So here's a fair warning if you're a rock junkie. Topsail is covered in these stunning smooth stones, and each one of them is going to call out to you. If you've forgotten to bring a bucket, you can stuff them in your bathing suit (which is my go-to backup plan). Be advised, however, that a breaking point does exist, and there's only so much spandex and elastic can do before they're going to throw in the towel. Buckets are best.

This showstopper Scotch bonnet was found by Joseph Fusco on North Topsail. When he heard I was writing this book, he put it in the mail as a gift because he wanted others to see what an incredible island Topsail is. The wise shellers are generous enough to share even their really special finds with others because they fully understand how Mother Nature works. By giving to others, the universe will open them up to receive more for their kindness.

Be careful at very high tides on Topsail Island. The ocean can come right up to the dunes, and there's no place for you to walk. When that happens, you can get caught in between the dunes (which you aren't allowed to climb) and the surging waves. The surf can sweep in very quickly and knock you down.

Holden Beach, North Carolina

Sometimes before dawn, giant Atlantic murexes like these will pop up on the berm on Holden Beach. Spotting their profiles down the beach with your headlamp and running toward them is a total rush.

It's time to talk about "Golden Holden." Back in the spring of 2022, officials in Holden Beach, couched between the Grand Strand to the south and the Outer Banks to the north, decided to renourish the beach by pumping in new sand. In Holden's case, the washout revealed seashells and fossils of such magnitude that nobody in the Carolinas had seen anything like it. The true seashell and fossil enthusiasts recognized how rare these finds were, and since then the masses have been flocking to Holden with very high hopes.

If you hit Holden square on the nose, it's possible to leave the beach with a handful of jewelry-grade shark teeth, a bucketful of sea biscuits, and a menagerie of other seashells that you just won't find with regularity at any other North Carolina beach, including rare flat scallops, lion's paws, and giant Atlantic murexes. The fossil record of the Cretaceous period that washed out during the 2022 renourishment is also remarkably interesting, so when the Holden waves recede, you are looking at the remnants of animals that lived 65 to 145 million years ago. You can't let the enormity of that pass without appreciating it. Fossil collectors at Holden regularly find the teeth and vertebra of mosasaurus and plesiosaurus, two massive wacky-looking water reptiles resembling lizards that swam in the ocean when dinosaurs were on the land. Holden also produces horse teeth, many extinct species of clams and oysters, and a variety of other unbelievable fossils.

One of the major draws to Holden for shellers across the country is the number of sea biscuits (echinoids) that routinely wash out post-renourishment. Just after the beach was refurbished, locals said the sea biscuits were so plentiful that dump truck loads of them were being scooped up and taken away from the beach for disposal. Even at the time of this writing, there are still people driving from many states away to try to find a sea biscuit at Holden. This renourishment washout has gained national attention, much to the chagrin of many of the local grumps, some of whom might bark at you during a chance encounter on the beach.

Even so, this flurry of activity at Holden is temporary because the material from any renourishment eventually washes away and gets picked. There will come a time when the chatter about Holden in the online forums will cease and the next trendy beach will take center stage.

If you're planning to road trip to Holden, know that there are not many hotels nearby. The beach was developed with a focus on houses instead of high-rises, which along with the blue-green hue of the ocean water is about 75 percent of the island's charm. Lodging will need to be booked through a realty company or a site like Airbnb or Vrbo. All of the seashell/fossil hype has pushed the rates up (particularly for oceanfront rentals), so be prepared for that. If you're going to the island just for the day, know that public parking is extraordinarily limited. The most popular place to park is at the pier

Flat scallops and lion's paws are a sheller's dream, and Holden Beach makes those wishes come true over and over.

(which is not operational), but the lot fills up very quickly, and you do have to pay. There are other smaller lots around the island, but many of them take you outside of the zone where the renourishment produced the best results. You want to concentrate your searching efforts between the pier and the water tower to the east and the pier and the Dolphin Street access point to the west. This is approximately a three- to four-mile stretch, which is very walkable over the course of a day. Unless you want to face the grim reality of a portable restroom, you'll be on your own with bathroom breaks at Holden, so be advised of that.

Photos like this one have affectionately been termed the "Holden handful." I actually found all of these teeth on the same day. This is also one of the reasons I don't usually take fossil excursions. There's really no need to pay for a charter that will give you a limited amount of time to hunt if you can figure out how to find things like this on a public beach.

The whole horse conch is a very rare find in the Carolinas. When I saw the tip of this Holden honeybun sticking out of the sand, I was jubilant.

This is one of the reasons "Golden Holden" is on the shelling map: the famous sea biscuits (or the "infamous" sea biscuits if you're one of the locals who is miffed about the thousands of visitors who come to the island just to find them).

Cherry Grove and the Grand Strand of South Carolina

Among shellers and fossil hunters, Cherry Grove has long been known as a honey hole. Some of the biggest shark's teeth you'll ever find on a beach are waiting there. Cherry Grove is home to perhaps the best fishing pier on the planet. It's worth a trip there in the summer if for nothing else than to sit on the end and observe the mackerel fishing. The locals know of a few sneaky (but legal) places to park for free, but you should plan to pay to park when you arrive. There's a convenient lot across the street from Boulineau's right where the Sea Mountain Highway intersects with Ocean Boulevard. The lower floor of the Prince Resort also has paid parking availability.

While Little River, South Carolina, is technically the top of the Grand Strand, Cherry Grove is the first beach access point on the sixty-mile stretch of coast known by that nickname. The Grand Strand includes North Myrtle Beach, Myrtle Beach, Garden City, Murrells Inlet, Litchfield, and Pawley's Island. Georgetown, South Carolina, is considered the bottom of the Grand Strand. The shelling and fossil hunting are consistently good for the whole sixty-mile length, though there are many considerations you should make before deciding where to go. If you're looking for a family-friendly environment, keep it low-key in Cherry Grove, Litchfield, or Murrell's Inlet. Be sure to check the events calendars for the locations you're considering because even the quiet spots can get a bit out of control during spring break, motorcycle-themed weeks, festival weeks, and holidays like Memorial Day, the Fourth of July, and Labor Day. Readers are strongly discouraged from hunting after dusk or before daylight in Myrtle Beach as some areas may not be safe. Don't even do it in a group.

The Grand Strand produces the largest quantity and highest quality of olive shells

The much-sought-after "Pawley's shell" is at the top of every sheller's bucket list while on the island. These imperial Venus clams are actually not that uncommon at other beaches, but I really like the fact that the Pawley's locals make such a big deal out of them. Every town should celebrate something so wondrous.

you'll find anywhere in America. On a day when the shell beds are cranking out large chunks of material, you can fill buckets with them. You'll also do well with shark teeth, fossils, and other varieties of seashells on most of these beaches.

We can't leave the Grand Strand without a quick aside about Pawley's Island, a quaint little nook you should make every effort to see in person. Aside from the ghostly legend of the Gray Man who has been alerting residents of impending hurricanes for the past two hundred years, the other thing the island is famous for is the Pawley's shell. It's an imperial Venus clam that can be found on other beaches, but the locals have adopted it as a mascot, and visitors always try their hand at finding one.

Grand Strand shellers continually keep an eye on the renourishment schedule for all local beaches. A 2022 replenishing project in Litchfield put it on the shelling map for many months, and the rumors are always swirling that Myrtle Beach is next in line for a dredging project. If you're planning to visit any of the beaches in this area, be sure to check on the status of these projects ahead of your trip. While they can provide advantageous beachcombing opportunities, they can also shut down the beach in front of your resort during a vacation.

Having grown up on Grand Strand beaches where olives are so plentiful, I'm always amused when I hear a Florida sheller get really excited about finding one. Almost everything in life is really about perspective. This olive shell is particularly noteworthy because you can see the ridge on the side where the animal had to make a repair after some sort of damage.

I always have good fortune with auger shells on the Grand Strand. They aren't as common elsewhere, and that conical shape is never going to go out of style.

The fossil forums are usually hopping with lofty tales from hunters who found "the big one" on the Grand Strand. These great white shark teeth were scooped up very close to the Cherry Grove Pier and were commemorated with all kinds of hooping and hollering.

It's rare for me to hunt a beach on the Grand Strand and not find at least one whelk. They're plentiful along this marvelous stretch of coastline.

Charleston, South Carolina, Lowcountry

The Lowcountry of South Carolina is known far and wide for its historic architecture, distinctive seafood-based cuisine, and shelling and shark tooth hunting. The region includes coastal counties like Charleston, Colleton, Beaufort (pronounced "Bu-ford" instead of "Bo-fert" like the North Carolina town of the same name), and Jasper. The Lowcountry's salt marshes and inland rivers produce some of the finest fossil hunting on the entire globe.

South Carolina's beaches are home to some devastatingly handsome moon snails. This one was my boyfriend for a while.

Both the Cooper and the Ashley Rivers flow back in from the ocean, providing endless opportunities for divers to find a secret spot very far inland. This particular stretch of coastline is peppered with satisfying beaches like Folly (which gets the most attention in the seashell discussion), Kiawah, and Isle of Palms. The most notable characteristic of the Charleston beaches is the seemingly endless pipeline of heavy-duty whelks that make appearances there. A lot of the shell hash on these beaches has a blue tint, which is just terrific. So the verdict on the Lowcountry is solid shelling beaches but fantastic fossil-hunting rivers.

Edisto Island, South Carolina

If you want to be left completely alone, turn off of Highway 17, head down Highway 174 under a canopy of live oaks until the road hits the water, and make a left into Edisto Beach State Park. You'll find peace and quiet there (along with some killer shells and shark teeth). You're going to want to make the 1.8-mile trek to Jeremy Inlet for the best shelling opportunity. That will require that you hang a left if you're looking at the ocean. Interesting finds will greet you along the way, but the inlet is really where the action is, especially if you can get there at midtide as the water is falling. As the tidal pools

The cockle is common in the Lowcountry. I picked this one up on the high line of a Charleston beach after it had been there all day with no takers.

While a lot of people spend time in Jeremy Inlet looking for shells, I tend to have the best results in the shell beds down closer to the ocean that run parallel to the inlet. That area is full of broken shell matter, but even in a spot that looks like a boneyard, there are whole shells hiding in there. As every minute passes with the receding tide, the water gets shallower, and you'll be able to see more in the tidal pools.

form, look in the water for the knobs of honking-big whelks sticking out. They're just everywhere down there and in unusual orange and rust colors that aren't as common elsewhere. You'll need to wear shoes with a good sole because the inlet has some oyster beds that are sharp, and don't underestimate the rigor of the walk. Remember, not only will you have to get there, but you'll be carrying a heavier bucket of shells on the way back.

Even though it's close, Edisto isn't technically considered one of Charleston's beaches. It's very good news that you don't have to get tangled up in Charleston's traffic drama to get there. Truthfully, the drive down Highway 174 is enough to make the trip even if you hit an off day with shelling. Edisto just feels like a different world. Ask anybody who has ever been there, "If you could only be on one South Carolina beach, which one would it be?" The answer will be Edisto every day of the week.

The ocean is just on the other side of this sublime oyster bed. Search the water right at the lip of the bed to find the whelks that rolled down and got stuck there as the tide receded.

If you want a sand dollar, Jeremy Inlet will probably give you one. This inlet is not stingy.

Tybee Island, Georgia

Some mornings you just wake up and need to see a lighthouse. Tybee Island, Georgia, has a stately one that will satisfy your hankering. When fellow shellers ask for Tybee recommendations, the best advice is parking on the north end and walking toward the lighthouse. The beach wraps around where the Savannah River comes in, and from the rock jetty on back the shelling is supercharged. Tybee almost always has some decent shell beds, but they just explode in volume (both high and low on the beach) once you pass the rock jetty headed inland with the river. You'll see gravel beds that are packed with shark teeth and seashells on the beach and larger things rolling around in the water too. The point with the lighthouse is a heavenly place to set up a little beach camp for the day and comb over the shells at your leisure. Tybee is known as "Savannah's beach," so everybody and his brother who wants a beach day comes out there. The drive always takes a lot longer than anticipated, so pack your patience.

The large white and gray shells in this Tybee shell hash are called ark shells, an incredibly common species on most American beaches. However, just because something is readily available doesn't mean it has no value. Just when you think you've found every color variation of ark shell, a new one will jump up and surprise you.

The tip of Tybee Island also has a rock jetty. It's a wonderful double whammy for shelling.

Golden Isles, Georgia

There's no place in the entire state of Georgia prettier than the Golden Isles. The region includes St. Simons Island, Jekyll Island, Sea Island, and Little St. Simons Island. The first Golden Isles exit off I-95 north is about thirty minutes from the Florida/Georgia line. This tiny strip of islands is less than a hundred miles long, but it contains about 30 percent of all the marshland on the entire East Coast. The Golden Isles is not the place for swimming because the area is a breeding ground for many species of sharks. They're literally everywhere, and watching the local shark anglers participate in the state's catch and release monitoring program is a fine way to pass a summer day. Sea Island is private and accessible only by residents, club members, and people with documented business there. Jekyll Island is gated, but anyone can pay a fee at the entrance and gain access. Of the three isles the public can visit, Jekyll is by far the best for shelling.

Jekyll is a top-three destination in the country if you want a place to consistently find sand dollars. You can park at any of the beach access points, but Corsair Beach Park right as you come off the causeway is an ultra-convenient

place to stop. Sand dollars abound there at the low tide line, but surprisingly a negative low tide doesn't help much because that just exposes a line of squishy muck that you really don't want to walk through. St. Andrews Beach Park at the southern tip of the island is also great for finding radiant whelks and other shells, but most of them are usually occupied and need to be returned to the water. When you visit Jekyll, take a bucket because you'll likely find as many sand dollars as you can carry. (And then have a tray or something to transport them home due to their delicate construction. They crack like egg shells if you look at them wrong.) Even if you're just travelling to or from Florida, Jekyll makes a great pit stop, only fifteen minutes off Interstate 95, especially if you're at the exit when the tide is almost low. It's a truly exceptional place.

Cumberland Island isn't technically part of Georgia's Golden Isles, and you have to drive to St. Mary's, Florida, to catch the ferry that will take you there, but you absolutely have to know about it. The island is inhabited by wild horses, the beach is pristine and empty, and many of the streets are paved with gravel that's full of shark teeth. Be aware, however, that you have to walk a long distance over dunes to get to and from the beach, and the heat indices are so severe in the summer that the dunes can be deadly if you don't cross back over from the beach before the peak of the day. Also be advised that there are armadillos out there that will chase you and not apologize for it. All in all, though, everybody needs to experience a beach so untouched and so full of shells.

If you ever have the opportunity to take the ferry out to Cumberland Island, Georgia, don't squander it. I believe there are certain places on this planet designed to settle us down. I always catch my breath when I'm on Cumberland.

If sand dollars were real money, this would be seven dollars in my pocket. Notice the variety of colors that dead sand dollars can have.

Add St. Andrews Beach Park on Jekyll Island to your travel agenda. It's a naturalist's paradise.

Take your cameras because every island in the Golden Isles is amazingly photogenic. Also don't miss Jekyll Island's Driftwood Beach, one of the most photographed locations in Georgia. I have never found it to be great for shelling, but many people love it there. This photograph was taken at the south end of Jekyll looking over to Cumberland Island, accessible only by ferry.

If you can't find inspiration in St. Simons Island, Georgia, you're a lost cause and we're going to have to go on without you. Even the fish are writing novels there.

Fernandina to Port St. Lucie, Florida

The real estate between Fernandina Beach and Port St. Lucie has some sensational beaches and many quality state parks, but the beachcombing is pretty basic and average. Fernandina is widely known as one of the best places in Florida to find shark teeth. From that point southward (including the Jacksonville beaches, Daytona, Cocoa, and so many points in between), you'll find lots of seashells. It's just harder to find anything really *special* in those areas. Because of this, it's not worth it to book a trip in any of these locations specifically to hunt, and most of the time it's not even worth it to make a pit stop if you're traveling along I-95 headed somewhere else. This is surprising to most people because on the whole Florida is the best shelling state in the continental United States. It just isn't productive on that east side until you get down to the Juno Beach area. That's where the good stuff will start calling your name as you zoom down the interstate. This whole swath of coastline is really the transition zone as Florida's waters get bluer and clearer the farther south you go. Say it with me: *Keep driving until the water is very blue and very clear.*

You'll find seashells if you hunt the Atlantic side of Florida from the Georgia line down to the middle part of the Florida peninsula. The terrific discoveries will be hit or miss, though, and for the most part you'll come home with shells that are common but still captivating, like this scallop.

Amelia Island's scenery is sumptuous, but it earns only a C- on its shelling report card. The beaches on Florida's east coast deliver much differently than the beaches farther south.

Palm Beach County, Florida

Florida's Atlantic coastline from the top of the peninsula working down is angled at a slant. In Palm Beach County, however, that slant shifts and bows outward instead. From the very point where that begins to happen, it's like the seashell faucet turns on full blast. Among all of those Palm Beach County communities, there's one clear frontrunner: Juno / Jupiter Beach. The seashells there are just epic, in both quantity and quality, so much so that many shellers don't even look for shark teeth because they're 100 percent distracted. The ocean is usually incredibly rough, so casual beachcombing at the water's edge in your street clothes isn't always possible. You'll be happier in swimwear so you can get into the ocean to grab the goodies that tempt you to go out a little farther in the surf with each new wave.

So much beauty is overlooked by hunters who have their vision focused on larger shells.

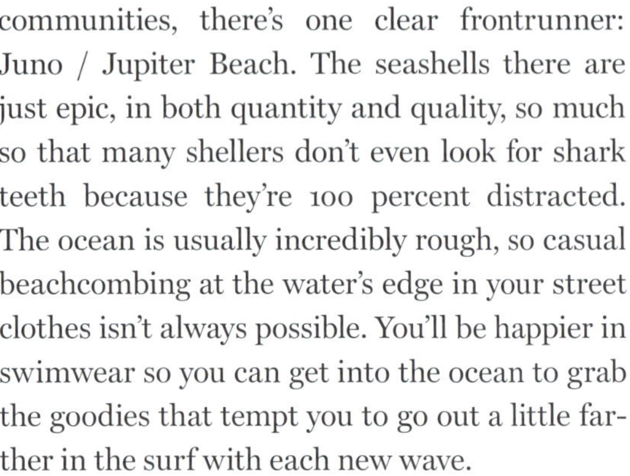

This specific stretch of beach from the Loggerhead Marinelife Center up to Jupiter Dog Beach with the pier in between is a fabled shelling hotspot. Think happy thoughts while you're walking near the pier because sometimes shelling wishes are granted in the form of rare sundials. Most beachcombers are elated to find one Scotch bonnet a year, but in this area it's possible to scoop up dozens on the same day. Olives abound, and there are frequently lion's

If you want Scotch bonnets, Jupiter Dog Beach has them. I once found thirty-two of them in an hour with my son, and it was just about the most fun I've ever had on a beach. They can be located in the water and in the shell beds (especially at the high wrack line).

paws and sometimes a helmet shell in the mix too. Large seashells are not on the regular menu in Palm Beach County, but that's okay because the appetizers that come in the small and medium variety are delicious enough to keep you satisfied.

Before we hopscotch in the next section down to the Florida Keys, it's important to mention Miami. Once you leave Palm Beach County, that geographical bow-out that was described earlier starts to curve around as the peninsula narrows at the entrance to the Keys and the Everglades. The shelling is just not the same at the Miami beaches as it is one county north, and quite frankly the prospect of Miami traffic is enough to make anybody's chest tight. If you have to have a nervous breakdown on the highway to get out to a beach, that's really just antithetical to the whole experience. Let the turnpike be your friend as you scurry around Miami and proceed onward to better shelling destinations.

Just a few minutes at Juno Beach can turn out a whole cache of unanticipated treats, like this spiny oyster.

Insider tip: While in Palm Beach County, adjust your eyes to focus on the micro shells and you might spot a coffee bean trivia. They're about the size of a sugar pea, and they look like little jelly beans.

The Florida Keys

Whenever shellers in the online forums ask, "Can I find seashells in the Florida Keys?," the locals almost always answer in unison: "No." It's a lie—all lies.

You can find incomprehensible seashells in the Florida Keys on both sides of the A1A (Gulf and Atlantic) and by both walking the beach and snorkeling near and offshore. There are thousands of things to love about the Florida Keys, but from a shelling perspective, what makes this 110-mile stretch of islands so special is that you can find species of seashells that are either rare or nearly impossible to find elsewhere in Florida, on the Eastern Seaboard, or on any other beach in America for that matter. Just a few hours of driving down from Miami, and you'll be in the land of queen conchs and cowries. The pieces of detached coral, nerites, and strapping Caribbean sea biscuits will keep you up at night thinking about the next day's beach adventure. Inevitably, when you're in the Keys, you'll find something you've never seen before.

When my dear husband says I shouldn't bring home any more sea beans from the Florida Keys, I just laugh and laugh.

Now there are admittedly not many sand beaches on your way down through the Keys, but that just means you have to preplan your stops if you aren't interested in snorkeling. Two favorites are Anne's Beach and Bahia Honda.

Anne's Beach is at mile marker 73 on Lower Matecumbe Key near Islamorada. There's very little designated parking, so that can be an issue on a busy day. While there, be sure to check out the highest dry wrack line from the last tide because there are often spectacular sea beans tucked in there.

For an extended shelling stop, put Bahia Honda State Park into your GPS. It's in between mile markers 36 and 37 on Big Pine Key, and it's a splendid place for beachcombing, snorkeling, and forgetting about your life for a little while. Aside from Anne's and Bahia Honda, your best bet for shelling outside of Key West will be to snorkel either just offshore or from a boat. There are some parts of the Keys that have that nasty sludgy seafloor that makes you feel like you're sinking. If you're unfamiliar with the area where you're planning to snorkel, be sure to go with a guide. There are areas that are protected marine sanctuaries with specific rules about collecting, so it's best to have someone knowledgeable in your boat.

Once you get down to Key West, everything is amplified—from the colors to the scenery to the varieties of shells you might find.

Key West is a very tricky place to shell, which is one of the reasons it's so captivating. Not very many people have solved its mystery. There are several beaches around the island that are good for shelling, including Smathers. Other little secret nooks are hidden away in places only locals know about, but those will remain nameless because they're notorious for having broken clear glass, rusted nails, and seriously hazardous debris.

By far the best place on the island to shell safely is Fort Zachary Taylor State Park, which you will access by driving through Truman Annex. The park is open from 8:00 a.m. to sundown, and paid admission is required. Don't leave your bags unattended in the park because they will grow legs and walk off. The beach itself is only about a third of a mile long, and it gets picked over within an hour of the park opening. For the biggest and best shells, you need to be first through the park on a bike (because bikes are admitted before cars). Once you pay, you have to pedal very quickly to the bike racks at the first entry point, lock your bike as fast as you can, and then run to the beach. You might see others running as well. If you do, go in the opposite direction to try to see the parts of the beach that haven't been scanned yet.

Due to the short length of the beach, that first rush is really over in twenty minutes. What's happening with the tides will determine your next strategy. High tide is always best at Fort Zach. You want to be there when the water

Many of the shells you pick up in the Keys will be occupied with live animals. On occasion you'll see a little set of eyeballs staring back at you like those peeping out of the bottom of the shell on the left. Shells with visible animals in the openings have to go back. Oftentimes you don't realize they have critters until you pick them up, but as soon as you know, gently return them to the water.

If you're a birder, your homework is to book a trip to Key West straightaway. The early hours are the quietest time of the day. That's when the best birds hang out in places that you can photograph and talk to them.

is rushing over the huge piles of coral rocks that are all over the beach. It all looks like mounds of white gravel. Your eyes need to be looking for color because the seashells that do pop out there are vivid. With a falling tide, it's worth it to keep parading back and forth over the rock piles as the water recedes. Be sure to also check the two ends of the beach because they are often very active. You won't walk away with a huge quantity, but some days the quality will kick you right in the head. Most of the shells there are minis, but every now and then a whopper will make an appearance. You do need to wear shoes the whole time you shell because the rocks will shred your feet. On a favorable water clarity day with no Portuguese man o' war warnings up, snorkeling for shells in the park can be fruitful too.

Fort Zach is also known for its collectible sea glass in really rare colors. Your pockets will be full of aquas and purples, not just ugly old brown. Also keep your eyes peeled for sea beans at the high wrack line in the seaweed.

Because of the illegal activities that sometimes take place in the Caribbean and southwest Florida, you need to be aware at all times and on any Keys

It was a good morning to walk in the Florida Keys—but then again, you have to work really hard to have a bad morning there. Caribbean vase shells, nerites, limpets, gaudy nauticas, and cowries abound, and the colors will sing you a tropical song.

Everybody who shells in the Florida Keys wants a queen conch. The juvenile shells like the ones in the picture will wash up on the beach occasionally. You have to be 100 percent sure your shell is unoccupied before you take it because possessing a queen conch shell with the animal inside is illegal, and I'm not coming to bail you out of seashell jail.

We all have that one particular harbor that speaks to us more than any other. For me that port is Key West. The island wedged itself deep into my soul on our very first rendezvous, and I haven't been able to shake it ever since. Everything in the Conch Republic unfolds in resplendent color, and its glory is magnified in the early morning hours when the light is just perfect and everyone else is still sleeping off the night before. The jetty at Fort Zachary Taylor State Park is the perfect place to count your blessings and to look for seashells tucked up in the cracks between the rocks.

beach that you might find *other things* out there. That's all I'll say about that (other than don't touch it, pretend it didn't happen, and get out of there lickety-split).

From start to finish, Key West is the ultimate paradise, and there will never be another place that resonates in such profound ways with its devoted followers.

The Everglades

There may be seashells in the Everglades. Who knows. Because there are alligators, crocodiles, rattlesnakes, pythons, and unspeakable spiders down there, none of us should try to find out. Just wrap on around the bottom of Florida and keep going.

If you do decide to stop in the Everglades, the signage indicates that it's frowned upon to feed the alligators sugar cubes with your hand very close to their mouths. Be advised.

The Ten Thousand Islands, Florida

Before you visit the Ten Thousand Islands to shell, your beachcombing life will exist in black and white. The first time you step off the charter boat onto one of these sublime islands and see the mass of shells spread out like jewels, it will all switch to Technicolor. The Ten Thousand Islands chain runs between the Everglades on the west side of Florida all the way up to Marco Island. The entire region between the Ten Thousand Islands and Sanibel Island is unequivocally the best place to shell on the beach in America. There's really no argument for anywhere else to take the crown.

Variety is the name of the game in the Ten Thousand Islands. Shellers will never stop flocking to this utopia. Each outing is like a scratch-off lottery ticket with the very best odds of winning.

What's so alluring about the Ten Thousand Islands is that the islets that compose it are accessible only by boat and there are endless places to land, so the chances of being first to a stretch of beach are significant. This region also grips shellers because of the startling variety of rare seashells that are found there and the sheer volume of other desirable species that are available.

You'll need either a private boat or a charter to access the Ten Thousand Islands. Some of the islands include Kice Island, Dickman's Island, and Shell Island. Many hunters also really dig Cape Romano. Most of the charters operate out of Goodland, Florida. The paid excursions are pricey, and parking fills up so fast there, but if you get a captain who lands you first on an island at the right tide, your wildest shelling dreams will come true.

This is what I mean by high volume and high quality in the Ten Thousand Islands. You might bring back several buckets like this from just one charter.

The tulip variety in the Ten Thousand Islands is world-class. No other region can boast of such largess.

Marco and Keewaydin Island, Florida

Marco and Keewaydin Island are neighbors with serious shelling swagger. These two islands are constantly on the radar of every calculating beachcomber. Marco is full of exorbitantly expensive high-rise hotels but a cool mix of restaurants and shops. There's quite literally nothing on Keewaydin Island, and you can get there only by boat. While the vibes of the two islands couldn't be any more different, what they share is the distinction for being in the top-five best shelling islands in America. Keewaydin gets the edge, but Marco is a fierce contender.

If you don't have lodging on Marco, the best place to park is at South Marco and walk toward the jetties. Be mindful that there are very few places in Marco to get off the beach because the resorts are fenced and gated, so

Marco and Keewaydin Island, Florida, have to be the best place for a newbie to get started with the hobby. All of the species you want to find are there.

Marco Island is famous for its rose tellins. It's the only island where I've ever found one.

pay attention to what your access point looks like. South Marco stands out for its rose murexes, and the island is known for its gorgeous apricot-colored rose tellins. At the northern tip of Marco is Tigertail Beach Park. The shelling is outstanding up there too, but you have to walk miles to get to the tip, and if you don't want to add extra steps to your hike, you need to cross an utterly disgusting squishy-bottomed moat on foot. Many people claim Tigertail as their favorite shelling beach anywhere, and a lot of junonias roll out there each year. Tigertail deserves the hype for its abundance of sand dollars, which can be found at low tide on Sand Dollar Spit at the point, and its huge whelks, which can be snagged by snorkelers on high visibility days.

Despite their close proximity, Marco and Keewaydin are really two different worlds. While there are a few houses on the western side of the island, the vast majority of Keewaydin is undeveloped. There are no bathroom facilities, no trash cans, no vending machines, and no lights. There are also basically no trees for shade, so nobody should visit without significant preparations. The only way to get there is by boat—a private boat/kayak, a shelling tour, or the Hemingway Water Shuttle. If you're unfamiliar with the region, renting a boat is not recommended because the waters there are ultra-shallow, especially at the low tides when you're going to want to go shelling. At some points your boat will be in only a few feet of water, and it would be very easy to run aground and damage your rental. Kayaking is a possibility, but this area of Florida is an unnerving place to be on the water in a very small boat due to the unexpected wind and weather changes and the amount of really high-speed motorized boat traffic. Additionally, if you miss your tide window in a kayak, you could be in for a long wait until the water turns in a more favorable direction.

The Hemingway Shuttle is the ideal way to see Keewaydin Island. That's why most of the tickets book up weeks and sometimes months in advance for the best tides. Fares are affordable, and the family who runs the shuttle and their dog, Captain Jack, are delightful. Be sure to choose your departure ticket and your return ticket at the same time. Booking with the Hemingway Shuttle allows you to stay on the island a lot longer than you would be able to with a shelling tour.

Getting to spend a few minutes with Captain Jack on the Hemingway Water Shuttle is worth the price of the boat fare. Your whole family will have a superb day on the water with such a good boy at the helm.

Keewaydin Island is the undisputed alphabet cone capital of the world. It might also be the undisputed champion of undisturbed beach beauty. Ravishing is the word.

You can also stay overnight and camp on Keewaydin if you arrive in a private boat. Be advised that camping out there is incredibly risky, though. The weather in southwest Florida is volatile and should never be underestimated. Significant storms can blow up out of nowhere. Even when you camp overnight in January (basically the coolest month), you might still get hot during the day. The heat would be unbearable in the summer, and seeking shade inside a tent would only make you hotter. You have to take a considerable

Both Marco and Keewaydin produce true tulip shells with the most fascinating colors and patterns. Imagine never finding a true tulip in your life and then landing on an island where they're everywhere.

amount of water to be able to sustain yourself for twenty-four hours or more. Many inexperienced campers have gotten into trouble on Keewaydin, including groups that have had their tents blown away by nighttime storm fronts they didn't anticipate. Another main consideration that needs to go into your planning is the bugs. They're appalling out there, and even if you're just day-tripping, you need to take multiple forms of bug repellent.

The reason beachcombers would even consider going to all of this trouble is the unimaginable scale of the shelling. It's truly off the charts. Keewaydin is most noted for the number of junonias and unoccupied giant horse conchs that are regularly found there. It's also the very best place on the planet to find alphabet cones. There is—hands down—no beach in America that will offer you as many cones as Keewaydin.

Before we leave this region, it would be a crime to skip over Bonita Beach and Lover's Key. Both are overwhelming in their beauty, and the shelling is top-notch. If you're going to be in the Fort Myers area, you want to take a field trip to both.

Sanibel Island, Florida

Oh Sanibel. Where do we start? When you call, we answer. We dream about it at night when we're home. We don't sleep when we're there because we're too excited to settle down. Sanibel has earned its reputation as the "Seashell Capital of the World." Even though the island was crushed by Hurricane Ian in 2022, the magic is still there, and slowly but surely she's getting back on her feet. The people who claim her as the best shelling location on the globe have a sound argument.

If you're on the quest for your prized junonia, Sanibel is where you probably want to center your search. So many great shells wash up on Sanibel because it's situated sideways in the ocean—a very unique geographic position.

There are three main access points if you don't have lodging on the island. Lighthouse Beach has a good amount of parking, and local shellers just rave about their finds there. This won't be a popular opinion, but the Lighthouse

Every time I book a Sanibel vacation, I can't stop giggling. The perkiest orange scallops live there, and I know they'll be waiting on me.

area is a bit overhyped. Its most prominent characteristic is a large tidal pool that forms in the middle of the beach, and it's not as pretty or as productive as other parts of the island. The middle segment of Sanibel along West Gulf Drive does not have public access, so shellers use hotel locations like Sundial and West Wind to mark where they found important seashells. Bowman's Beach is the next public access point. There is parking, but you have to walk quite a distance to get to the beach. Bowman's is better than Lighthouse, but with a choice you should keep driving toward Blind Pass. Though it has a tiny parking lot, Blind Pass is the most advantageous place to situate yourself on the island. You can still walk back toward Bowman's if you want, but there's usually no need because you'll find a bucketful of happiness very close to the Blind Pass parking lot. Overall, there isn't as much parking on Sanibel as there is demand, so be sure to get there very early and be ready to pay way too much for your parking space.

From Blind Pass, you can look across to Captiva Island and the Turner Beach parking lot, which is also tiny. Captiva

Blind Pass never sleeps, and the second that there's any sunlight beginning to glimmer behind the palm trees, the parking lot is packed with a line of cars waiting.

When people in the shell forums ask if the "shell piles" are out, this is what they mean. Strong Sanibel surf action will cause piles of shells to accumulate around tree roots.

I truly don't understand how anyone who is fortunate enough to live on Sanibel Island ever gets anything done. They must be ruined by the beauty that surrounds them. How would you even be able to motivate yourself to mop the floor or report to work when the seashells are laying out there just begging to be found? Pictured above is a fig shell, a species that's abundant on Sanibel.

is actually prettier than Sanibel, though the shelling is not quite as strong. Many of the shellers who book lodging on Captiva end up driving down to Sanibel to hunt there. The parking rates for some lots on north Captiva are fifteen dollars an hour, which is ludicrous. Among the two islands, Blind Pass and Turner are the first in class for shelling.

The possibility represented in this picture is enough to drive just about any sheller into a fever. Miles and miles of the best shell hash in the world await you. Every beachcomber is offered something special on Sanibel. Nobody is left out when such an unprecedented volume of seashells is available.

Lighthouse Beach isn't my normal Sanibel hangout, but I will give it credit for putting this enchanted blue moon snail in my hands. The magic dust never fades away on a shell of this caliber.

Siesta Key and Lido Key

Sarasota County has some fine beaches to keep you occupied on the Gulf side of Florida. Siesta and Lido top the list, and the amount of conversation about the two in the seashell discussion pages confirms them as the heavy hitters in the area. Lido seems to offer up the spiniest spiny jewelboxes anywhere around, and dapper dark olives sun themselves on the beach on Siesta. You'll have to navigate some part of Sarasota to get out to them, with Lido offering the biggest traffic hassle. Many shellers talk about Turtle Beach on Siesta Key as a prime place to go hunting, but others find it to be underwhelming. If you're in the area, you'll be better served to shoot north to Siesta where the beach is much wider and prettier and the shells are more plentiful.

South Lido will always hold a special place in my heart because it's the site of my first whole junonia find. I celebrated by taking a screaming victory lap around the beach and then making a snow angel in the sand.

The Siesta Beach community has created really convenient public access points. Every time I have visited, parking has been a breeze, and the multicolored lifeguard stands just add an extra special touch to the scenery. You can tell when a town has thought through the details, and Siesta Key definitely has.

If you're moving north, you'll have to go back inland to get out to Lido from Siesta. The southern tip of Lido is terrific, so invest some shelling time there if you ever get a chance. You can either take one of the parallel parking spots on Benjamin Franklin Drive and walk on the beach to get south or park at South Lido Key Beach Park and walk straight out. You want to make your way to that south point because the shelling possibilities explode there. Focus your attention on that curve where the waterway comes in because breathtaking things roll around in knee-deep water in that precise spot.

Siesta Key has the darkest olives I have seen anywhere in my travels. They will turn you into a highly selective olive snob once you've seen them.

Even though Lido is very well known in the shelling community, I often find that I have it all to myself in the early morning. I really love it just before first light on a cloudy day because the intense blues and greens just don't play out in the same way at any other time. It feels like you're living in a painting that's still being created. Every frame changes second by second as the sun rises.

They grow their alphabet cones BIG *on the Sarasota beaches. Most of them come in this caramel color due to sun bleaching and age. When they are inhabited by the animal or if you find them shortly after they were vacated, they're darker in color and called chocolate cones.*

Pass-a-Grille, Florida

Pass-a-Grille is one of St. Petersburg's beaches, and it's the last way station on your northern Gulf trek in Florida that's really notable for shelling. There are some other sensational beaches on the St. Petersburg Peninsula (with Clearwater and Treasure Island among them), but the shelling scepter belongs in Pass-a-Grille's hand. The first time you visit, you might not hunt for the first few minutes—you'll be in awe of how beautiful the ocean is there. Pass-a-Grille is known for its junonias, so watch for the spots. Your best shot at premium shells will be at low tide because there isn't a whole lot of beach left at high tide in some areas. Parking can be limited, and since you have to get involved with either Tampa or St. Petersburg's unpredictable traffic to get there, taking a detour off I-75 for a quick visit isn't advisable unless you can arrive really early in the morning. One of the stand-out features of Pass-a-Grille is its shell hash. There are some spirited colors in the mix. As well, if you hit it right, you'll probably get into some sand dollars at PAG, which is shelling lingo for this terrific beach.

Several shelling charters go out of Tarpon Springs in the northern part of Pinellas County, but after that you'll run into a beachcombing dead zone as you skip around the Big Bend. That area is characterized by shallow not-so-pretty water with little wave action, and many of the beaches are marshy, rocky, or covered in oyster beds. There are a few dots of barrier islands accessible by boat, but you aren't going to have much shelling fortune otherwise.

The Florida fighting conch comes in so many colors. While they're very common on the Gulf side of Florida from the Ten Thousand Islands up to Pass-a-Grille, sometimes the pattern or color of one of them will still get me all tangled up in love.

If you want to make a dramatic and quick impact on your shelling capabilities, practice on the beach by allowing yourself to bend down to pick up only things with bright color. With enough repetitions, you'll condition your eyes to be drawn to the most coveted shells, like this juvenile horse conch. Cute as a bug in a rug.

Pass-a-Grille will hit you hard with sand dollars. Be ready for it.

Cape San Blas, Florida

Once you get through the Big Bend area of Florida, the first beach that again gets spunky with shells is Alligator Point. The landscape there is beguiling, and you'll find some exemplary things to put in your bucket. The stretch of Highway 98 from Lanark Village down through East Point is simply marvelous. It runs right by the water for miles, but keep trucking because Cape San Blas will almost be in view at that point, and that's really where you want to be.

Once you enter the T. H. Stone Memorial St. Joseph Peninsula State Park on Cape San Blas, you're going to want to drive up to access point 3 to park. Looking at the ocean, you'll walk to the right as far as you have the stamina, knowing you have to walk the same distance back. The trek to the point is about ten miles, and you may not encounter another soul at any point along the way. It's a harsh beach environment that should not be underestimated, but the shelling will knock your socks off. When you first arrive, you might not be optimistic about the way the shell hash looks. It's deceiving, so don't give up. Even if there's nothing pleasing at the low line, there are all kinds of beauties tucked away on the high line in the windblown dry sand. You're likely to find Scotch bonnets and nutmegs and at least junonia pieces. Many of the shells you'll see at Cape San Blas are broken, but if you stay the course you'll stumble upon whole ones too. The cape also has a strong sea bean game. If you can't make it out to Cape San Blas for whatever reason, St. George Island just offshore from Apalachicola is often in the shelling conversation and worth a visit as well.

I found several juvenile horseshoe crabs on the beach the last time I visited Alligator Point. This one was expired unfortunately. It's sad when they don't make it, but that's the circle of life.

Carrabelle, Florida, on Highway 98, can deliver a sunrise and a half.

Panama City to Pensacola, Florida

Once you reach Cape San Blas, you'll experience good shelling beaches all the way over to Mobile Bay in Alabama. This span of coastline includes heavy hitters like Panama City, Destin, and Pensacola. The ocean water turns a triumphant aqua blue, and the sand looks like granulated sugar. It will take you about two and a half hours to drive from Panama City to Pensacola, and within that distance of worthy beaches is one superstar that shines above all others: Navarre Beach. The sign coming into town proclaims it's "Florida's Most Relaxing Place," and the local chamber of commerce just might be right.

After you have that first opportunity to get acquainted with Navarre Beach, you're going to want to stay in touch. For those with only one shot to shell on the panhandle of Florida, Navarre is where you stop. You can drive across the causeway on Highway 399 and roll straight into the Navarre Beach Fishing Pier parking lot. You'll find yourself in a land of sugar-white sand and clear water with the most intriguing seashells rolling around at your feet in the surf. Sometimes the hype for a shelling location in the online forums isn't warranted, but in Navarre's case it definitely is. In just a thirty-minute walk, shellers will see Sozon's cones, flat scallops, and sand dollars. And you'll find other delicious beaches with noteworthy shelling opportunities as you move west, including Pensacola, Perdido Key, and Gulf Shores once you cross the Alabama line. But if you have only one wager to make, let it all ride on Navarre.

Every time I visit the beaches on the far western panhandle of Florida, I always stop and hold a handful of the sand. After traveling to beaches all over America, I can say without reservation that I've never seen sand more appealing anywhere else.

You know you've found the right beach when you walk out, look down, and immediately pick up a flat scallop with such vivid colors. Navarre for the win.

If Navarre's sand doesn't steal your heart, its aqua blue waters will.

Navarre doesn't always produce a high volume of cones, but it often delivers some of the more unusual varieties. Pay close attention to the shells you find there because you may walk up on something super rare.

Dauphin Island, Alabama

So this one is a pretty big secret: Dauphin Island, Alabama. Of course, residents in the state know it's spellbinding, but most beachcombers outside of Alabama have never heard of it. In fact, the majority of people really stop thinking about the possibility of good beach finds in the Gulf once they pass the panhandle of Florida moving west. Don't discount Dauphin. If you're on I-10 between Mobile and Pascagoula, pay attention because you don't want to miss your turn.

With mega-resort beaches like Gulf Shores just across Bon Secour Bay, it's hard to imagine an uncommercialized and perfect little island like Dauphin is right next door. If you're a bird watcher, this place will blow your mind. Dauphin Island is the only place outside of Florida where you can see such a variety of shorebirds. The Dauphin wildlife is so photogenic,

One of the factors that goes into choosing my shelling locations is how far I'll have to walk until I don't see any more people. That's the goal: salt, sun, sea, and solitude. In Dauphin's case, the answer to the distance question is happily "not far."

you won't know where to point your camera first. When you hit the tide right, the shelling can be epic. It's a stretch of sand that always produces something interesting, whether it's shells or shark teeth. Sand dollars also proliferate on the island.

Because it's mostly private residential, there aren't a ton of places to access the beach. The public beach park is in the middle of the island, and while it does require quite a walk to get out to the beach, it's a satisfying hike, and you get to walk across an old pier. West End Beach (which was closed for several years after Hurricane Ida wiped it out in 2021) is a favorite among beachcombers. When you first arrive to that beach access, you'll see a glut of people as you walk out. Keep hiking, though, and before long it will be just you and the crabs. (And a word about those crabs—they are the pushiest ones you'll ever find on any island. Hundreds of them will stand

This enormous ray mouth plate was such a surprise on my first visit to Dauphin. I knew instantly that the island was going to be my friend for a very long time.

in the road and block your car early in the morning, and they will not be the first to flinch.)

There are a few affordable inns that are very doable for a short stay, but they book up way in advance. The Gulf Breeze Motel is a joyful place to spend a weekend. Add Dauphin Island to your "must visit" list. You won't regret it.

Hunting Like a Boss

Getting Up Early

Veteran shellers get up and go early because the ocean consistently delivers amazing things in the morning. There's no time to brush your teeth or comb your hair. You don't snooze for five more minutes. You go. This is not to say that you can't find anything good on an afternoon tide. It's just that the afternoon is when everyone else is on the beach, and you aren't going to have a private showing of the shell beds. If you have a choice, early is always the answer.

You can sleep when you're dead. Go experience as many early beach mornings as you possibly can.

The early risers get not only a front-row seat for the best sunrises (like this one near Daytona Beach, Florida) but also access to the top-shelf valuables Mother Ocean deposited overnight.

Pink sky at morning, sailors take warning. Cherry Grove, South Carolina, regularly puts on head-turning sunrise displays. Seeing them is worth more than getting a few extra hours of sleep. Mother Nature seems to pull out her best paints and brushes in the morning. Today's canvas will never be replicated in the same way. Don't miss it, no matter where you are.

Dedicated beachcombers are usually the kind of people who put off their own needs when the opportunity for choice hunting is there. We walk even if we're hungry or thirsty. Even though we may need caffeine or a bathroom break, we push through. It doesn't matter that we're sleepy. When you have the passion, that takes precedence over what else you might need or want.

If you're one of those people who consistently sleeps in, that probably means you're going to consistently miss the morning window of opportunity, despite how much you want to become a better sheller. If you have to dilly-dally around the house, brew your coffee, and think about things before making a move, the best shelling will be over. By the time you get out there, the people who were first will already be back at their houses drinking their coffee and cleaning their extraordinary treasures. And if the lure of shelling alone isn't enough to rustle you out of bed earlier, the glory of an early morning sunrise should be added incentive. If it somehow turns out that you don't like all you see and feel out there on a clean, fresh morning, you can go back to hitting the snooze button, and we'll leave you alone.

Reading the Beach

Every beach is going to give you signals about what's happening that day. The more perceptive you can train yourself to become, the better you'll get at reading these signals. This skillset is called reading the beach. Once you're proficient at it, your assessments will become automatic. If you're just learning how to do this, below are some questions that will help jumpstart your thinking about what you see on the beach.

1. Is there a large quantity of shell hash or a good number of shell beds on the beach?
2. If not, can you look down the beach in either direction and see any shell material in another location?
3. If so, is that material big and fat or fine and grainy?
4. Are there shells rolling around in the water?
5. As you take a first look at the shell hash, do you immediately see any whole seashells, or are they mostly broken up?
6. Do you see any really desirable seashells or shark teeth right away?

Worm snails are easily broken because of their tubular construction. When I find a whole one in a shell bed, it's usually a good indicator that other whole shells are in the area.

The optimal condition that you're looking for is a beach covered with shell hash when you look both right and left, and you want the individual pieces of that material to be as large as possible. If it's a good shell washout (a layer of material that has just been exposed for the first time), you'll begin to see the shells you want right away. It's almost always a positive harbinger for the day when you can walk out and immediately start seeing whelks and other sizable shells.

When the conditions are prime, you want to put yourself where the newest material has been revealed by the ocean. By paying attention to where the sand is wet (and by knowing the tide heights for the beach where you're looking), you can determine the limit of where the latest high tide line went. Unless you're searching right after a hurricane when vast swaths of the dry sand on the beach might have new shells mixed into it, hunting the super-high line is likely not going to be productive because those shells have been laying there for a long time. (You can often tell because they're really dry and sun-bleached, and you can see a ton of footprints in that loose sand.) Even yesterday's high tide line (if it was higher than today's) has been thoroughly picked over if you're on a popular shelling beach.

If a whole bunch of big material has been exposed, you're likely going to be dealing with a wrack line full of debris and seaweed. Carefully move that stuff around with your foot or with a shelling scooper because sometimes really neat things get pushed to the high lines and buried under garbage. More specifically, shells with big apertures—or shell openings—are shaped in a way that water gets caught in them. Their round shell bodies then roll to the high line from the force of the water. About 95 percent of the Scotch bonnets are to be found at the highest line because of the shape of their apertures.

Your assessment of the beach when you first walk out might reveal a high volume of shell hash that's fine and grainy instead of hunky and chunky. Shell hash that's really broken up might produce small shark teeth and mini shells, but it's unlikely to produce the high volume of the shells, teeth, and fossils that you're there to find. In that instance, your reading of the beach may help you determine that you need to move to a different spot.

The pro hunters can take the reading of the beach to really profound levels with their ability to recognize fairly subtle nuances that give them details that inform their hunt. For instance, the appearance of squishy sediment balls is a strong indicator that the present washout is brand new (and experienced shellers know their eyes might be the first to see it all). The balls are like tar because they stick to your feet and shoes if you accidentally step on them. Whereas most people groan when they realize it's a tar ball day, you should get really excited because you've recognized the correlation between their appearance and the special seashells and fossils that often hang out with them.

Experience can also teach you how to read the specific species that are washing out that day. This analysis is very keyed to location, though. Banded tulips and nutmegs, for example, are fairly common shells in southwest Florida. However, finding them is pretty rare on the Grand Strand in South Carolina. If you're hunting in Myrtle Beach and start to see them, that shell bed should command your full attention.

The two shells pictured above are the banded tulip on the right and the nutmeg on the left. Finding them in Myrtle Beach is a tell-tale sign that it's going to be a banner shelling day.

The discovery of specific fossils is also a really important piece of information to add to your analysis. Seasoned hunters walking on the beach together sometimes talk about how they like the look of the shell hash as they approach a shell bed. If you've spent enough time in those concentrations of shell and fossil material, you learn to recognize the characteristics of the productive and unproductive beds.

You can also take a step back for a macro look at all of this. While shellers do read the beach when they arrive, there was a ton of "beach reading" involved in all of the decisions that led them to this part of the coast on this particular day. All of the strategies outlined in the first part of this book really are about reading conditions. It should be clear to you by this point that successful shelling is not dumb luck. The high-achieving shellers aren't just in the right place at the right time. They worked hard to figure out where the right place was.

Sometimes reading the beach is just a matter of spending a minute or two investigating the high wrack line. If you see only really common things (like this run-of-the-mill clam), you'll know that looking elsewhere might be more worthwhile.

This picture represents what I call a "game face" scenario. Sometimes you catch a break, and the whole beach is covered with shells. You can tell as soon as you walk out that today's the day. Therefore, you need to kick it into high gear and quickly cover as much ground as you can.

Shelling Speed

One of the most common pieces of bad shelling advice is to slow down and take your time. To the contrary, you have to *speed up*. If you've managed to arrive at the beach in the middle of the night, and it's just you and the birds, your goal is to cover as much real estate as you can before everyone else wakes up, especially if you're dealing with a lower tide. There may be a lot of exposed beach with new shell beds that nobody has searched yet. The big coveted shells—your giant conchs, whelks, and helmets—are going to be obvious. Their profiles stick out on the beach. If they're there, you'll see them—and so will everybody else once they arrive. You didn't wake up at 2:00 a.m. to find little shells, did you? No, you did not. You woke up in the middle of the night to fill your bucket with amazing things. To accomplish that, you have to *move*.

Here's how the pros do it. They often cover five to eight miles of distance in the night scooping up the big shells, many of which never make it to sunrise. Their pace is very fast—sometimes almost a jog. They make the first pass on the beach at a lightning pace. The walk back is for slowing down and meandering. That's when they'll have the advantage of some daylight to comb through the shell beds looking for the smaller things they passed over earlier. There's nothing inherently wrong with walking slowly. It's just that the time for walking is not first thing on a falling tide.

If you arrive at the beach at a higher tide when there is less exposed ground, you don't have to move with quite as much speed because you won't have as much square footage to cover.

Being able to move at a fast pace and maintain that speed for many miles does require a level of physical fitness. Many of the best shellers train for long-distance endurance even when they aren't at the beach so they can keep up with the morning shelling rush. Your daily exercise routine should include as many miles as you would walk if the shells were hitting. That way, when it's showtime on the beach, you won't peter out. The free health app on most smartphones will help you track your distance each day.

My family recently had the opportunity to hunt Blind Pass Beach on Sanibel Island. The three of us arrived at 5:00 a.m. for a 5:20 negative low tide. There was a lot of open beach and a ton of tempting shell beds because the winds had been incredibly strong the day before. I immediately found a colossal horse conch and knew we needed to make tracks to see what else might be laying on the beach in plain sight. My husband and son were inclined to stay very close to the parking lot and comb through the shell beds. I had to light a fire under them to move because I knew we had only a few minutes before other shellers arrived. After much cajoling, they finally listened to me, and just a few dozen yards down the beach from the shell beds they wanted to search was another really obvious horse conch and a whole bunch of mammoth whelks. If we had stayed put, we would have missed them. There was another pack of shellers who arrived about twenty minutes after us. Once we covered the majority of the beach heading up toward Bowman's, we then returned to those tempting shell beds at the retaining wall and spent time looking through them for the smaller shells.

Move! Go! Get it first! The early morning competition is absolutely fierce, and if you arrived first you want to maintain your positional advantage on the beach.

Putting in the Time

"I went shelling for thirty minutes and didn't find anything. I'm just not as good at this as you are." The epic haul pictures you see other shellers post online didn't happen in thirty minutes. Some were achieved by walking all day (beginning before sunrise and continuing until right before sunset). Just as moving quickly increases your coverage of the beach and thus offers you more opportunity to find seashells, so too does staying out there longer.

In most cases, the pictures you see in the seashell forums of massive payloads are the result of shellers who walked for hours and hours. Perhaps most importantly, those folks have probably searched the beach hundreds of times

Shelling well usually doesn't happen in an hour. It's a daylong investment. And even if I wasn't finding a whole lot, I would have probably still been out there the whole day. Think of this time commitment as putting in the reps like an athlete in training.

before when they found absolutely nothing. Those off days usually don't get posted on social media, so keep that perspective.

Putting in the time means that a sheller might make the commitment to drive long distances to get to a worthwhile shelling beach. For example, if you're in Orlando on business, you might get up at four o'clock and drive two hours to get out to Pass-a-Grille. It's a time suck and terribly inconvenient, but that's how amazing adventures happen. Just because you're not technically visiting Pass-a-Grille doesn't mean that it isn't within your reach if you're willing to dedicate the time and to tolerate some Tampa traffic. There's also a real possibility that you could drive all that way and come up empty-handed. After all, every beach trip is a gamble.

Sometimes the shellers who get a lot of attention online have their successes diminished by comments like, "You just have to be the luckiest person on the planet to find things like that." Those comments are actually backhanded insults that need to be corrected. The talented shellers and fossil hunters are actually some of the most dedicated people on the planet because they endure a lot of uncomfortable conditions to do what they do, and they're never deterred by the off days. You make your own luck through preparation and hard work, which, if you think about it, is what the first third of this book was about.

Walking the Shelling Grid

One of the most useful and efficient strategies that will help you maximize your time on the beach is called grid walking—to ensure you don't miss anything, you walk in a grid pattern, particularly when the shell beds have been pulled down by the tide and there's a vast swath of material in one place. If you walk in a straight line through it, you'll not get a thorough look at the majority of what is there. Remember, you want your eyes to pass over as many shells as possible during your walk to increase your chances of finding the most covetable ones.

When you're making your fast morning passes and trying to cover as much ground as possible, make a wide zig-zig pattern through the shell beds. At that point in the day, you're on the hunt for the hefty shells and shark teeth,

Don't be distracted by the glorious clouds in the photograph. What you need to see in this picture are the heavy shell lines that basically cover the whole beach. You would short-change yourself by walking through these beds in a straight line. With thick concentrations of shells like this, you want to see it all. Walking in a zigzag pattern will allow you to achieve that.

and you'll easily spot those. You can tighten up the grid in areas where the shell beds are dense. If you're in an area of the beach where there are few shells, you don't need to grid walk at all.

Unless they're headed back to their car with full bags, experienced shellers rarely walk in a straight line on the beach. If something catches their eye, they'll scoot over to it. Sometimes even after they look and walk away, they'll get a gut feeling that they need to go back and inspect the item more closely. If you're blessed with that intuition, always listen to it.

If you arrive to a beach hours after the high tide, chances are the higher line has already been picked over by previous shellers. In that instance, there's no need to include that upper line in your grid. Focus instead on the lower areas closer to the moving water that have been more recently revealed by the ocean.

Watching the Waves for Rolling Shells

Here's a real insider shelling secret for you: the vast majority of the big shells never make it to the beach. If you watch the waves breaking closest to the shore, you'll see them rolling around at the trough, or the lowest part of the wave. Most shellers on the beach aren't looking there, though. You really don't even have to be in deep water to snag them—you just have to be fast. If the waves are strong enough, the big shells can hit the sand and then roll up. The receding wave will usually take them right back down, so you have to pounce quickly. Be careful with your footing if there's a dip into a tidal pool right where those waves are hitting. The dip can cause the water to land with some force, which could sweep you off your feet and suck you and your cellphone out to sea. Follow me for more tips learned from very hard experiences.

There are some shells that are just built like a tank and won't roll in the surf, especially if their apertures are filled with sand. You can still see their profiles as the waves break, though, and that's when you have to go into ninja mode to retrieve them before the next wave surges.

Digging, Sifting, and Raking

There are a lot of people who love digging, sifting, and raking on the beach, and this chapter is likely going to irritate every one of them. For the most part, these practices are a colossal waste of energy. The ocean does the work for you. Every single wave rolling over a shell bed offers a new landscape to examine, and all you have to do is stand there. By now you also know that successful shelling strategy revolves around giving yourself the opportunity to view the largest percentage of material that you can in the shortest time frame possible.

Let's pretend you're going to dig yourself a hole for an hour. Even with a big shovel, you're only going to get so far. Everything you pull up is going to

be covered in sand, so looking at it all is going to take some time. Within that hour, after using all of that muscle, your eyes have probably scanned only a few bucketfuls of material. If you had spent that hour moving and letting the waves not only shake around the shell hash for you but also keep it clean from sand so you can see it easily, your eyes would have scanned a volume of shells measured in dump trucks instead of buckets, and it would be a smart bet that both the quantity and the quality you retrieved would exceed what you would have found digging. The more volume you see, the more potential you have to find. Shelling is absolutely a statistics game.

The same is true for sifting, especially if you're picking up handfuls and sorting through them piece by piece. You might stumble upon a shark tooth in there, but you're guaranteed to find more by walking.

Raking is a strategy that can be more productive, particularly if there are big shells rolling in the tide that you can't quite reach before the water takes them out again. This is especially true if the whole beach is empty of shells. If you have a rake, you can make your own fun. You're still stuck lugging around the goofy thing, though, and you'll shell more effectively when your hands are free. In the event of an empty beach, digging a hole at the edge of the water can also create a new shell bed, but you can really do the same work by jumbling up the sand with your feet. There are times when digging on the tips of islands (even if it doesn't look like there's anything out that day) can be worth your time, but digging really shouldn't be your front-line strategy.

It's important to acknowledge that many shelling enthusiasts sit and dig on the beach because of mobility issues. They really want to be moving (because they recognize the shelling advantage), but they physically can't do it. If that's

Why you don't need to rake: exhibit A—the ocean has already spread it out for you.

No need to dig! All of my finds come from the surface. The seashells are laying right there in plain sight. Use your energy to walk instead of digging, sifting, or raking.

you, this chapter is in no way disparaging that activity. There's a whole community of shellers who find it relaxing to sit and dig all day. It brings them great joy, and that's what this hobby is all about.

If you're going to dig, sift, or rake, there is some etiquette you need to follow. It's really jerky to dig a big hole and leave it. Those holes can also make it difficult for sea turtles to get in to lay their eggs or tend their nests at night. That said, as a walker, it's ultimately your responsibility to watch for holes even at night. There are also many diggers who get territorial over their holes, which is utterly absurd. If you dug a hole on a public beach and are in it, most people will respect your temporary right to dig in the space you created. But if you leave, that's no longer "your hole." Lots of squabbles ensue over this issue in the forums. You don't own the beach or the barrier island, so you have no claim to an abandoned hole. If you see someone going to the effort of raking out a big area of the beach looking for shells, try to honor their hard work and not stand below it to take advantage of the material washing out. There's plenty of room for all of us, so don't encroach.

Maximizing the Benefit of Moving Water

When the water is actively washing over a shell bed, there will be a lot of material floating and moving. That's when you need to be there. This area where the water meets the land and the wave loses its force is called the swash zone. It's only a few inches deep, and it's a great place to see seashells rolling and shark teeth shining.

Once the water loses it connection to the bed while receding or completely covers the bed while it's rising, your window of opportunity will close because that shell bed will stop rolling around. The faucet turns off, and sometimes you can almost pinpoint when it happens down to the minute. At that juncture, you'll notice that only a fraction of the material that was visible in the water is still there. Instead of a dynamic environment where each new wave produces another opportunity at discovery, you will move into a stagnant phase where all that's available is stationary on the beach. That area will get harvested quickly, and there'll be nothing new to see until another tide transitions that part of the beach into an active zone again. Once the faucet turns off and you feel like you've looked the beach over, that's when you go home. Invest your time and energy when the conditions are beefed up.

The productive times of finding lots of treats in the surf are always short-lived, so if you identify a shelly place, stay there because it'll likely fade away in a few minutes. You have to capitalize while it happens. If you're in a satisfying pocket that the water is churning, try not to make a big deal out of it and call attention. There's no shame in keeping it on the down-low.

The area of exposed beach in this picture isn't the only good place to be looking. Those first few inches of water create an ever-changing landscape that keeps everything underneath in flux. You can see that movement of shell material in the water and often spot and scoop up the shells you want before they are exposed on the dry sand.

The swash zone is a prime location to train your eye to the distinctive roll of certain seashell species. The alphabet cone, for instance, will do a wobble roll as it's moved around by the water because of its conical shape. Flat shells like scallops will float in on a wave. Practice in the swash zone to get your eyes accustomed to distinguishing these characteristics.

The swash zone can also be a cool place to use your feet to feel around for large shells that might be partially buried. So many incredible things get pulled up by shellers who were just using feel to identify buried targets underwater.

I see treasure in the swash. Do you?

Identifying Pusher and Sucker Tides

Sometimes without any discernable reason, Mother Ocean decides to pull every single shell, shark tooth, and piece of debris down off the beach. The not-at-all-scientific name for this phenomenon is a sucker tide. King tides that recede down to negative low tides can often pull so fast and hard that everything gets sucked down with the receding water. It's disappointing to arrive at the beach only to realize that a sucker tide has befallen you, especially if you got up in the middle of the night to commute. Unfortunately, there are many people who make long journeys to hunt well-advertised beaches, only to then take to the forums to air out their grievances when they find nothing. Nobody can control it, and no beach will deliver a successful walk every time. If you do happen to be in an area filled with shells on an incoming tide when a sucker tide starts to take shape, it's actually pretty fascinating to watch it pull everything under. But if you've just driven from Ohio to Florida to find seashells only to discover there aren't any there, it's understandable how the fascination wouldn't hit you quite the same way.

The equally nonscientific name for the opposite of the sucker tide is the pusher tide. Pusher tides are a sheller's best friend because they shove material up onto the beach and expose new shell material. They are responsible for those glorious shell beds that we love so much we could roll around in them.

You'll find that having a name to put to the disheartening tides will help you cope with the letdown, even if it's just a made-up name.

When you experience a pusher tide that makes the shell beds thick, one great strategy is to look for color among the more neutral hash. There are a few exceptions, but almost all of the shells most people really want to find are more brightly colored than the majority of the material that's on the beach.

Behold, the shell pile! This photo is from aptly named Shell Island in the Ten Thousand Islands chain of Florida. It's a bird nesting area that has boat landing restrictions during certain seasons. When landing is allowed, these piles will keep you happily occupied all day long.

Recognizing the Competition

The great movie icon Ricky Bobby once famously opined, "If you ain't first, you're last." The beachcombing competition is real—especially if the pros got out there ahead of you. Your goal should always be to get the first look. Especially in the early morning hours, you should scope out who is on the beach to determine if the heavy-hitting hunters are there. There's no need to be rude or anything, but do try to pick up the pace to get to the superior hunting areas first.

I am your competition. Look alive because it's time to rodeo.

In their formative hunting years, many shellers often get frustrated when they arrive at a beach really early only to see somebody else's footprints. Over time they learn not to be discouraged. Those tracks could have been laid down by someone who was just walking a dog. (You can look for the little paw prints to confirm.) Those footprints could have also been left by someone simply exercising and not beachcombing. Sometimes tracks are just evidence of a more inexperienced hunter who came before you and technically had the first look but left a lot of prizewinning finds behind.

When you see the prints, also pay attention to where they are on the beach. It may be that those people were out earlier than you but the tide was covering the lower part of the beach when they were there. If the tracks don't dip down to where you are, you might still be first to search that area.

After that first morning rush wears off, do your best to slow down and enjoy the experience without being so concerned with what others are doing. When you have a strong game, you'll find your share without having to be all hyped up about it. There really is value to being first, though, so pick up the pace, slow poke.

Slow and steady might win the race in other arenas, but it doesn't in shelling. Go, go, go!

If you team up with a capable shelling partner, you'll be able to cover twice as much ground in those early hours when competition really matters. Just make sure your buddy understands the mission and isn't going to crap out on you or complain the whole time.

Wading to Sandbars

Depending on the geography of where you're hunting, there may be sandbars that get exposed at lower tides. This is especially true on the Gulf side of Florida. These sandbars can act as a "second beach" because there's a whole new set of material rolling around out there, particularly on the ocean side of the bar. You'll often see expert shellers making a beeline for the ocean-facing edges of sandbars to look for giant whelks and horse conchs. Sandbars can also be excellent hunting grounds for sand dollars.

Even on days when big shells might not be rolling on the beach, there's sometimes great action out on the sandbars. Just be aware of what the tide is doing before you venture out to a sandbar and watch the clock while you're there so the tide doesn't strand you in deep water. Wild currents can also develop around sandbars, and danger that was not there when you waded out can reveal itself on the new incoming tide.

If you're bored on a sandbar, it's truly your own fault. There's so much life to see out there. If the currents are safe, you can also snorkel around the edges of sandbars where the water is shallow.

Searching Tidal Pools, Tree Roots, Berm Walls, and Rock Jetties

Watie's Island, South Carolina, is a privately owned and completely undeveloped beach in Horry County. It's covered in the most mesmerizing driftwood on the Carolina coast. Always take the time to look under every nook and cranny for seashells when you see driftwood like this.

A charter captain in southwest Florida once offered the best shelling advice when he learned that many in his boat were on the hunt for jumbo horse conchs. He explained that once the boat stopped moving, shellers needed to make a break for the driftwood and tree roots and start looking for the big shells that roll under there and get wedged. Sometimes only the tips were showing, and often the brown color of the periostracum, or protective outer skin, of the horse conchs made them blend in with the bark of the trees, but they were there in abundance. Be sure to give large pieces of driftwood your attention as you're working your way down a beach. So many shellers pass by buried gems that are waiting there.

Features like berm walls and rock jetties are also important places to investigate because they act as mechanisms for collecting shell piles when a pusher tide is cranking. If those walls and jetties are at the end of an island, all the better. Island tips where rivers and inlets meet the sea are very important places for shellers to visit. However, be advised that the moving water at the juncture points of islands and waterways is often where the food chain is most active. It's why so many people fish there. As well, any of the natural and manmade features discussed in this chapter can create unpredictable currents that make the areas very dangerous for swimmers. Even

This is the horse conch, one of the prized finds on most shellers' wish lists. This particular example is occupied by a live creature and needs to be left undisturbed. The empty horse conch is among the bigger shells that can roll in the surf and get jammed under driftwood.

if you don't intend to swim, strong ocean currents in even knee-deep water can be enough to knock you off your feet and take you away from the shore.

Tidal pools should also be on your radar because big shells sometimes roll over the ocean-side lip on an incoming tide and stick in there. Likewise, the dip of the beach-side lip on an outgoing tide can be a place where the big shells roll down and get partially covered. You can feel when the energy of a receding tide stops sending waves over a tidal pool. Those first few minutes are the best time to grab shells in the pool before anyone else.

If you plan to do any water shelling near inlets, rivers, berms, or rock jetties or in water that might contain tree stumps or large pieces of driftwood, you must wait until the sun comes up for safety. The currents in these special areas are very inconsistent, and what felt safe one day might not be the next. There will still be plenty of shells in the water at sunrise. Pictured for attention is this pretty little sunray Venus clam.

As you can see from this chapter, the successful calculus of the really strategic shellers involves so much more than just walking by the ocean and hoping luck will intervene. By building your knowledge about the sneaky places where fetching seashells might be overlooked by other shellers, you'll be ready to use all of the features of the beach to your full advantage.

Honey hole tip: There's always something shaking at the rock wall in Pass-a-Grille, Florida. Many shellers in the area start their hunt there and then proceed north to scan the rest of the beach.

The jetty on the north side of Tybee Island, Georgia, is an ideal hunting location. You can see all the gravely goodness that the tide is pulling down in the foreground here. That shell hash is full of fossil shark teeth, while the big shells likely wait in the water where the wave is crashing.

OPPOSITE: *Tidal pools are an excellent place for new beachcombers to practice seeing shells in still water. Once that skill is developed, it's easier to identify the same species in a moving tide.*

Finding a Honey Hole

Certain stretches of coastline continually produce blockbuster shells. When you get really familiar with a beach over time, you'll figure out where those places are. On South Marco Beach in Florida, the series of jetty walls that you'll see to the left once you go out at the southernmost access point is a consistent shelling spot. Under and near the fishing pier at Juno Beach in Florida never disappoints. The area a hundred yards to the north and south of the pier at Cherry Grove in South Carolina has an endless supply of fossils and seashells to offer. Tigertail Beach in Florida and Jekyll Island in Georgia will always kick out sand dollars. It's literally impossible to put your toes in the sand and not find something awesome in Dauphin Island, Alabama.

Those honey hole locations are often guarded by the people who know where they are. There's a fringe element in the beachcombing community that will simply never tell you where they were. These coy hunters exist in the rock, fossil, arrowhead, sea bean, sea glass, and sea float forums, in addition to the shelling groups. The easy fix for them should be to not post what they find so that nobody asks the location question. Sometimes this secrecy rises even to the level of online bullying when they attack someone for unknowingly naming what they perceive as "their spot" in public comments. Territorialism is very distasteful, and those who do waste mental energy in playing this kind of constant defense are really missing out on the joy of sharing what they know with someone who wants to learn and have great experiences.

Sometimes the honey holes are not location-specific or consistent. You can just find a span of ten or twenty-five yards of beach on a given day that's dropping wonderful shells like a loose slot machine. In mere minutes the action may fade, so when you find those, stay there and enjoy the moment. It's often the case that small pockets like that will produce a few tides in a row, so always check back on the following day. You'll feel such a sense of accomplishment by being persistent and finding those sweet spots. Coming back to them is like visiting a loyal pal.

I'm often asked about the location of my favorite shell hunting spot. I've had ongoing love affairs with many beaches, but Keewaydin Island, Florida, tops the list. The picture above is a typical scene at the water's edge. I spy with my little eye another cone that needs to come back to my house. And this photo reminds me that it's time to book another trip.

Beach Hopping

This chapter blows the lid off a pretty well-kept secret among proficient hunters: we beach hop. We don't stay on a beach that isn't generating results. In fact, some of us might hit four or five beaches over a fifty-mile span all before the sun comes up on a single morning. If after a quick read of the beach we determine that the hunting isn't going to be constructive, we leave. For instance, there are shellers who will stop at nearly every beach access point on Ocean Isle Beach in North Carolina before they find a satisfying shell bed.

The reason this information is such a secret is because usually your only window into the world of these expert hunters is through their social media posts, and they don't post when the hunting goes cold. Therefore, couched between those two posts of picnic tables filled with glorious seashells might

Don't settle for a beach that isn't giving you what you want. You have to know when to cut bait and try something new.

be nine days with no posts. Those nine days likely represent unfruitful days searching. They still went, they just didn't hit the jackpot—because nobody does every day.

If the sun isn't up yet, you still have time to leave the beach you're on and find a better one before everyone else wakes up.

If you visit a location and use the beach reading strategies discussed earlier in the book or if you're in a place where the hunting just isn't working, leave that beach and try somewhere else. When you've rented lodging for a week to specifically hunt for shells and the beds have just not popped out, drive to another place. Especially if your vacation will be ruined without a memorable experience hunting, it's worth it to pay for an Uber to get to a more productive beach. You can also see if your hotel has a shuttle available. Sometimes if activity is slow, the drivers will take you somewhere other than a designated stop like an airport, especially for a generous tip.

Beyond beach hopping when we aren't satisfied with the day's results, proficient shellers tend to adopt a mindset geared toward exploration. That impulse toward adventure compels us to take tons of day trips and invest hours and hours of travel time to access the beaches that intrigue us. For many beachcombers who are just learning about the hobby, their concept is framed within their weeklong annual vacation. Because of this perspective, they often don't understand why they don't find seashells like the ones they see in the Facebook posts. The reason isn't that they're ineffective hunters; the great posts are just created by people who drive all over the place all the time, and even if they live pretty far inland from the coast, they devote many weekends to travel just to have a few hours exploring a new beach.

To be a successful seashell hunter, you have to be flexible when your plans fall apart, and diligence is required in trying to come up with an alternative course of action. You're guaranteed to find nothing if don't try again. Your results will definitely improve as you increase the number of beaches you add to your rotation.

Assessing Water Clarity

Water clarity is a measure of how far you can see in an ocean or river. It's controlled by how much stuff is in the water and how the ocean is shaking it all up. Water clarity is profoundly important to shell hunting success. With no visibility, the water hunting component of your game is taken completely out of the equation. Even in the shallow waters of Florida, with poor water quality, you won't be able to see through even a few inches of water to the shells on the bottom. On the days when the water is clear, you can walk out for dozens of yards and see the ocean floor just as clearly as if there was no water at all. Water clarity is a vital factor even when you're just hunting in the swash zone.

Storms and hurricanes will mess up your visibility in the water, sometimes for very long periods. Intense hurricanes can leave the ocean churned up and brown with debris for weeks or months. Red tides and algae blooms can be equally bad. On days when water quality is especially poor, snorkeling for shells isn't possible.

Those with vast experience navigating the ocean can read the environment

and make determinations about what the water quality will be like. Most knowledgeable anglers can do it too, and they have cameras they can drop from their boats to see what the water looks like that day. It's fine to just show up at the beach to see what unfolds, but be prepared to get in the water and snorkel or just stay on the beach depending on how clear the ocean is.

One of the many reasons I love shelling in the Florida Keys is because the water clarity is usually good in the shallows where I hunt and snorkel. This is Bahia Honda State Park between mile markers 36 and 37 on the A1A. Even if you're on the way to somewhere else, it's worth the stop to walk around in the clear water for a few minutes. You'll feel better about things if you do.

On high-visibility days, the shells on the ocean floor reveal themselves as if there is no water over them at all. This picture was taken on an exceptional water clarity day in Sanibel Island, Florida. It looks like a Florida fighting conch committee meeting to me. The two banded tulips must be guest speakers on the agenda.

Hunting at Night

This chapter opens up a big old can of worms because night hunting is a complex dichotomy: it's both rewarding and risky. You'll find incredible things out there while everyone else is asleep. If you consider night hunting

from the standpoint of competition, it's obvious that covering eight or ten miles of beach before the world wakes up will be advantageous. Once daybreak approaches, the other shellers who think they're early by arriving at five o'clock will begin to stir. That's usually when the night-hunting vampires are leaving the beach with very full pockets.

It's always beneficial to beat the crowds. If you're searching a busy beach in the summer, there may be two hundred other sets of eyeballs scouring the sand just within fifty yards of where you are. In the middle of the night, your peepers are the only ones in the game. Everything that's there is going home with you.

The best strategy for night hunting is to arrive at high tide and stay there for the whole falling tide. When giant whelks, conchs, helmets, or murexes have popped up, they'll be really obvious, and you'll see them easily. Likewise, megalodon and great white shark teeth will raise their little hands and wave at you.

You'll obviously need high-quality headlamps and flashlights with batteries that will last at least six hours to hunt at night. While you're out there, be sure to scan your lights back and forth as you move so the light hits the beach at varying angles. Sometimes the profiles of the big seashells are not visible if you shine the light one way, but if you move and sweep your light a different way, they'll come into focus. If there's any kind of hump or slope on the beach you're hunting, be sure to continually look behind you on the ground you've just covered because receding tides can sometimes sling really big shells up on those banks after you've already walked through that area.

It's a good idea to scope out where the shell beds might be emerging the day before you plan to hunt at night. Knowing that piece of information will tell you where you need to be at about what time in the tide. Always return to beds that have produced previously because they tend to yield again and again.

Before you decide to hunt at night, though, you have to be a capable hunter *in the daytime.* The skill of training your eye has to be developed under the easiest condition: bright sunlight. Once that light is taken away, you're hunting in a tunnel because your scope is limited to only where your light is pointed. Night hunting is enormously difficult. It takes some seasoned daytime hunters five or six years to master it, and some never gain proficiency because it requires very sharp eyesight. As you're learning, be prepared for some ungodly wakeup times that result in mostly empty shell bags. Don't be frustrated as you're teaching yourself to hunt at night, though, because it's a skill acquired with practice, and it's a mighty fine one to have in your arsenal.

Perhaps the best part of night hunting is the solitude. It's a really special thing to walk in utter silence for four or five hours and not have interactions with any other human. Your brain waves will open up under an enormous full moon over the ocean. Hearing the crashing surf but not seeing it is like an elixir. There are so many impressive birds and an array of other animals

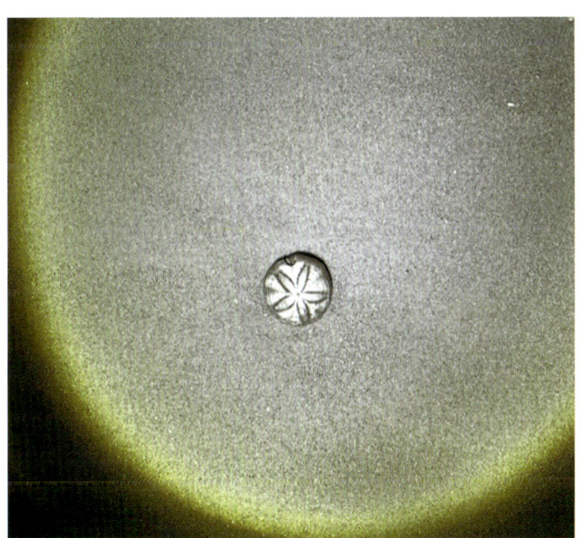

Night hunting isn't the lemon in everybody's tea. It requires a lot of dedication and skill development over time. At night you'll be able to see only the area right where that circle of flashlight beam hits, so it's much like hunting in a tunnel.

It's surprising but ultimately true: Once your eyes are acclimated to hunting by flashlight, you'll be visually drawn to color even when you're surrounded by pitch-black darkness. Those daytime hunting skills will translate once you have your bearings and feel comfortable out there at night.

out there that you never see during the day when the beaches are crowded. Pulling up a surprising seashell in complete darkness all alone is absolutely surreal. It's the closest you'll ever feel to Mother Nature's comfort.

The enamel on big shark teeth catches the glow of the flashlight in a very distinctive way. Once you learn what it looks like, you'll be picking them up like Easter eggs.

The wonder of this isolation is not shared by everyone, however. Many people are freaked out by being that alone for that long. Instead of a calming effect, night hunting is a stressful experience for those who can't suspend their worries about the risks long enough to enjoy themselves. While being out there alone and in the dark is wonderful, it can be dangerous. If you're going to try night hunting, consider going with an experienced friend first until you learn the ropes. It's also imperative that you read the chapter on beachcombing safety before you attempt it. With the great reward of being first on the beach comes a whole heap of risk that you need to consider.

Putting All of These Strategies Together

A Keewaydin Island Story

The first half of this book has thrown so much information about strategy at you that it's critical to pause here to review how all of this works together. Instead of thinking about these techniques in a vacuum, the next step is to consider how they work in tandem. This is essentially the crux of what the expert beachcombers have figured out: how to form a synergy among a lot of moving parts and develop a singular plan of action tailored to an individual day. The best way to illustrate this is with a personal narrative.

It's the seashell to beat all seashells. My son found this stunner on Keewaydin Island, and we were all just speechless.

Our family had been on the hunt for a whole junonia seashell for years, but it had always eluded us. We found cobbs, which have broken or chipped outer layers but still have the spiral inside, and we found pieces, but never a whole junonia. This necessitated the development of a very strategic plan.

First, years of research revealed that Keewaydin Island, Florida, was statistically one of the best places on the planet to find junonias. By watching the shelling forums month after month and by paying attention to where Js were popping up, the best search location became readily apparent. A scouting trip to Keewaydin on the Hemingway Water Shuttle allowed us to gain familiarity with the island and its hunting conditions. We had a terrific shelling day, but no junonias

The point of Keewaydin Island where the Hemingway Water Shuttle drops off is maybe the best shelling location I've ever discovered. At low tide, there are holy grail shells everywhere. Even with the sun up, you can see from the photograph that there was no competition. Just look at all of the large shells scattered about.

emerged. There was stiff competition out there that day, which was a prime indicator that for the best shot at this shell, we needed to be on the island when nobody else was. The first privately owned boats and kayaks tend to arrive around 7:00 a.m., and the charters start to come about an hour later. The only way to beat the crowd was to arrive by private boat and camp. Now, I'm not the kind of girl who sleeps outside; I need outlets, high-thread-count sheets, a white noise machine, and preferably my cat to sleep well, but I was determined that this would be the year of the junonia. So with that the first two factors were solidified: we had a location and a plan for reducing competition. The more difficult component of the equation was yet to be answered: when to go.

We learned in an earlier chapter that the currents are stronger in the winter months, and thus the shelling is better. As well, in southwest Florida the negative low tide is when the magic happens. The next skills that needed to be applied were reading the tide charts months in advance to pick a winter day when the water would be at its lowest while coinciding with a full moon. In booking lodging and transportation that far ahead for a trip, you can only hope for favorable winds, which happily materialized for us. At this time in 2023, the Ten Thousand Islands were also still experiencing above-average shelling conditions post–Hurricane Ian. It was a quadruple victory: negative low tide on a full moon with an already stirred-up shell situation in the winter.

After arriving on a Friday, we set up our camp and waited for the negative low tide the next morning around 4:30. It was a stellar shelling day that included a Scotch bonnet, several flat scallops, and more empty horse conchs than we could carry. We were literally leaving them behind. The excitement was so overwhelming that I couldn't sleep. I stayed up all night shelling for what ended up being more than forty-eight hours without rest. (Later when I told a friend about this, she said, "Oh Ash. You do know that the military keeps recruits in boot camp awake for two days straight to try to break them, right?" And there I was intentionally doing it for seashells.)

My son, who was eleven years old at the time, got up around 4:00 a.m. to join us for the hunt. The water went out so far on that negative low tide that it felt like you could walk into the ocean for a mile. There were live shelled

This is why we need to talk about shelling, to share strategy, and to give up our honey hole locations. Every family deserves to find this kind of bliss outside together. Our kids must be allowed time to be beside the water so the glory of the ocean lodges deep into their spirits. They're going to need its solace in this crazy world we will hand off to them one day.

creatures everywhere, and it was just bewitching to walk among them as the only humans there. It was our own private island. And that's when I heard my son's excited voice pierce the darkness from a few yards away: "Mama! Mama! Mama!" I knew exactly what it meant: he found a junonia. And it wasn't just any junonia; it was the most exquisite one I had ever seen. There aren't words to adequately describe the exhilaration that silly shell brought to my family.

What I want you to glean from this story is how to make this kind of experience happen for yourself. Through much careful thought, I was able to pick the right location, tide, season, and moon phase. I reduced our competition. We made sacrifices with our comfort to camp. We stayed up all night to catch a very early tide. In a nutshell, we put all of the pieces together. You can do it too, with research and preparation. Set a goal of finding your own once-in-a-lifetime shell, and get to work figuring out the logistics. Believe it will happen, and it will be so.

Continuing to Build Your Skills

These shells are called flamingo tongues, and they were found in the Florida Keys. It's fairly unusual to see them with any peach color left. They're commonly sun-bleached (like the example on the right).

Training Your Eye

We all know those people who just seem to have an uncanny ability to spot rare things like Indigenous arrowheads, four-leaf clovers, and shark teeth. Despite the prevailing belief, they aren't just lucky. They have trained their eyes through years of practice. This is precisely why they can often walk through a picked-over shell bed and find things that others left behind.

Effective shell hunting is a cumulative skill. The more you find, the better you will be at finding. If you're willing to continue practicing, you'll be a better sheller in a year than you are right now. The reason is that over time, you can teach your eyes to see anything you want to see. You might hunt for years on beaches where junonias are often found but never hit the jackpot. Once you do, however, your eyes will be accustomed to their distinctive spots, and

Once you've trained your eye to recognize the distinctive features of shells, shark teeth, and fossils, you won't need to see the whole thing before your eye registers what it is. I knew this was a sand dollar because my eyes are attuned to the floral design even if it's partially obscured.

you'll likely come across more. All it takes is that first experience to show your eyes what their assignment is.

The process of training your eye essentially comes down to repetition. The basketball players with the best free throw percentages are the ones who for years stood out on their driveways at night and wouldn't go inside until they hit a hundred free throws in a row. You'll be glad you were persistent on your quest when your moment finally comes. Some elements of your beachcombing game will develop more slowly than others, and training your eye is one part that might take the longest.

When your skills become noticeably better, it will then be easier to add new species to your repertoire. Also remember the advice from the earlier chapter about buying specific shell species that you most desire. That at-home visual aid will be an essential part of your training process in preparing for the field.

The white stripes and the pointy spires of the king's crown are the peculiar characteristics that you want to encourage your eyes to gravitate toward.

Color is probably the most important facet of a seashell that will help you distinguish it from the less sexy shells on the beach that don't warrant your attention. And shoot, was this scallop sexy.

Hunting Inland Rivers and Creeks

So far we have focused exclusively on surface finds on beaches, but this text would be remiss if it didn't highlight the enthusiasts who do their hunting entirely under water. Millions of years ago, the ocean used to cover almost half of North and South Carolina. The Sandhills were actually the ancient ocean's coastline. Therefore, all of the seashells and fossils from the long-ago animals who lived during that time can be found on that Sandhills land through excavating. The same is true of many other parts of the coastal United States. The easiest way to access those old fossil layers today is to let inland creeks and rivers wash them out for you. By exploring creeks and rivers, pedestrians with no scuba or snorkel gear can find outstanding fossils from digging on the banks and sifting in the muddy water. Those with the necessary experience can also dive the rivers, some of which are quite deep due to dredging for ship traffic, to look for their loot, and those underwater finds are sometimes just inconceivably good.

One of the main reasons creek hunting on foot isn't appealing is that poisonous snakes and alligators abound in these areas, and to hunt this way you have to be willing to spend the day in the mud with no ocean view. In the summer, it may also be obscenely hot without an ocean breeze. As for the river hunting, you must be very experienced and capable to take on the challenge. Even those who are dive certified don't need to be splashing down in Carolina rivers willy-nilly because the currents are unbelievably strong sometimes, and there are a lot of underwater hazards that can tangle your dive gear. It takes a long time to learn how to read these rivers for risk, so doing so under the supervision of a very experienced river diver is critical. If you watch the fossil pages, you'll see the posts about divers who went

This is why the divers face the risks. A selection like this can come up with an inland river diver after just an hour down below.

Justin Kiser is a reputable fossil dealer who owns an Etsy store called SharkToothShackSC. There you can find astonishing fossils that he brought to the surface at a price well below what many other dealers ask. When you buy, tell him Dr. O sent you.

missing, were severely injured, or lost their lives in these rivers diving for fossils and seashells.

If you're ever fortunate enough to go out on a river dive boat, the experience will give you a totally new perspective on the risks that divers take to recover underwater shells and fossils, the amount of work that it requires, and the financial expense. You'll never complain about the price of diver-located seashells and fossils again. Justin Kiser is an experienced diver in the Cooper River in South Carolina. All it takes is a few minutes listening to Justin converse with his dive partner to be totally blown away by how many factors they have to consider as they decide when they should go out, where they should stop, and which specific place is safest for the dives. This is all irrespective of the preparation that has already occurred in relation to safety planning in the event that something goes wrong while they are forty feet down.

There are several excursion companies that will take you out to dive, hunt the creeks, or search other inland sites. Be sure to check out the social media presence of the people and companies you're booking to see how they speak to others online. Some of the land and creek excursion guides are among the most territorial people you'll ever encounter. You want to ensure that your dollars aren't supporting online bullies or those who are repeatedly caught for hunting on private lands without permission. You could get in trouble for booking a trip that takes you to land where you're trespassing. There are legal places where the public can hunt without having to pay anybody to help. For instance, Green Mill Run in Pitt County, North Carolina, is a creek that's commonly hunted by sifters who bring up real-deal fossils and shells. There are many other areas like GMR, as it's known in the forums, where similar honey holes are to be found. Go if you wish, but if a creepy crawly gets you, you were warned.

After seeing the lengths that diver Justin Kiser went to in order to bring this five-inch megalodon tooth to the surface, I'll look at every diver-direct fossil I purchase in a fresh light. If you disagree, buy a boat, fill it with gas, outfit it with safety gear, secure insurance, buy a full set of diving garb and tools, go down a time or two in zero visibility with the gators, and then we can circle back around and see if you've changed your mind.

Until you've been on a Lowcountry river in a boat, it's impossible to fully recognize everything Mother Nature is doing out there.

Taking Shelling Excursions

As global ecotourism continues to grow, there are more people each year who want to include some kind of nature-based adventure component to their travels. Shelling excursions are wildly popular in America, and there are some really outstanding charter companies that provide incredible experiences your family will remember for a lifetime. As with all things, though, there are advantages and disadvantages, and that's how we'll consider whether going on an excursion is right for you.

Advantages

Shelling and fossil tours flourish in areas where there are "secret" locations, and the tour companies know where to take you. Your access to their expertise can be vital to your success, particularly if you're hunting in an area where you don't have familiarity with the surrounding islands.

People sometimes find astonishing things on paid charters. These businesses have an easy time promoting themselves on social media with pictures of what their passengers find. You should follow a few of their pages if you're considering booking a charter to get an idea of what to expect.

Some islands are too dangerous to navigate on your own. While you can rent your own boat to explore barrier islands, in places where the water is very shallow, the negative low tides that you want for hunting are times when the boating conditions are absolutely treacherous. If you don't know where the sandbars are or what the navigational signs mean, you can easily run your boat aground. There are times in the Ten Thousand Islands in Florida when captains are running in about a foot of water. Maneuvering a boat out of really shallow water after you have shelled an island can also put you in a pickle that you might not have enough boating experience to wiggle out of.

You get a lot more than just shells on the excursions. Tour guides will often take you to see wild horses on local beaches on the way out to your excursion destination. Some of them know where to find dolphins that will swim and leap behind your boat. Being able to leave the main tourist beach areas behind and going out on the open water adds significant value to the excursion.

Disadvantages

Some shelling charters are very expensive, even when your experience isn't private and you're on an excursion with other parties. From the perspective of the owner running these charters, that expense really isn't excessive. They are, after all, having to supply the boat, pay for the insurance, meet the Coast Guard's safety requirements, and, most importantly, offer their time and expertise to help you find things. From the beachcomber's perspective, if the charter turns out to be unproductive, it can seem like money that wasn't well spent. If you regularly take charters, there will definitely be times that you disembark from excursions wishing you had saved your money instead. Remember that just like a regular day on the beach, the barrier islands sometimes have off

Charter clients want prize shells (like this flat scallop and Scotchie found on an excursion in southwest Florida). Results like this are never promised, but with enough research you'll begin to notice the captains who make it happen for their guests more often than not.

days too. It's still frustrating to realize you've just spent three hundred dollars or more to find that out.

If your boat arrives to a destination after another company has already landed, they may have "cleaned off the beach" ahead of you. Because many charter companies are allowed to leave docks only at certain times, it's possible for kayakers and private boaters to get out before daylight, and when the extra low tides are happening in those hours around sunrise, the earlier birds are going to get most of the worms. A fast-moving party on your own boat could even get out ahead of you and take the premium shells. And the charters don't always depart on time. They will sometimes wait for a tardy party to arrive, and because they usually have other groups lined up for the rest of the day, those lost minutes might not be added on to the end of your excursion (not to mention that you might be missing all of the primo goods while you sit there due to someone else's poor planning).

Your time on the excursion is limited, and that pressure is sometimes a distracting feeling, especially if you aren't finding much and you can feel the clock ticking. On three-hour tours, you'll likely spend a lot of your time looking at your watch. If the commute to the destination takes thirty minutes, that leaves only two hours to search, which means you can get only an hour away from the boat before you have to turn back.

It isn't fun when you've paid for an excursion and you get a captain who isn't very knowledgeable. It's a rare occurrence because excursion companies don't stay in business very long when their reviews are poor. In areas where lots of charters operate, word gets out about which companies are the most user-friendly and deliver the best experiences. While there aren't too many companies with *bad* captains, you might get a charter with a *new* captain who isn't fully up to speed yet on species identification or one who takes you to an island that has not been producing in the previous days.

Some dig experiences are highly expensive, and they sometimes plant shells and shark teeth for customers to find, which is a real letdown for true hunters who want to find things in situ. The recommendations in this book should put you on a free beach where you can find your own fossils that are of equivalent quality and quantity to those found at inland dig sites.

Most experienced shellers and fossil hunters book tours and excursions only selectively because they have learned where the best car-accessible locations are. However, if you want to experience a charter or excursion, do your research in advance. Some of the most reliable charters are the ferries

If you're weighing your options for a paid excursion, consider whether there's a comparable beach you can access for free. In a lot of cases, you can find one.

that will take you from one location to another but won't actually provide a guide (like the Hemingway Water Shuttle to Keewaydin Island, Florida, or the Shackleford Island, North Carolina, ferry that runs out of Beaufort). Look for ferries and charters that have been in business for a long time. Read their reviews and talk to other shellers about their past experiences before you invest. You can also call many charter boat captains directly to get a sense of their personality and the vibe of their company. The ones who are jerks usually show their true colors early in the conversation. Many will not answer the phone while they're out on the water with clients, so leave a message.

Staying Safe on the Beach

In a perfect world, we would all be able to enjoy our beaches without having to think about risks. The reality is that all beaches are inherently dangerous places, and we should have our guard up all the time. As hunters, we're in a constant state of vulnerability because our hobby requires us to look down. We're often not conscious enough about scanning our surroundings for what might be watching us. The ultimate goal is always for you and your family to have a terrific time at the beach and leave without incident.

Some of the safety issues discussed in this chapter are commonly known. Meanwhile, there are many risks that folks might not have considered before. Please read the whole section and recognize that there are dangers in both the daylight and the darkness. We shouldn't go forth in fear, but we should be smart about our choices.

All beaches are home to predatory animals, and you need to be prepared to encounter any species at any time. If you're hunting any coastal area in the United States, you should to be aware that at any point you might encounter a bobcat, rattlesnake, alligator, coyote, bear, panther, or mountain lion. There are panther signs in some coastal areas of southwest Florida and black bear signs throughout the Big Bend area. Though the official position of many state wildlife organizations north of Florida is that big cats like panthers and mountain lions are not in existence, there have been many credible sightings accompanied with photographs that have been reported but not accepted and then verified. State wildlife managers issue habitat location maps every few years denoting the areas where they're confident that predatory cats reside, but it's also fairly small-minded to say it isn't possible for animals to move outside of those shaded bubbles on a years-old map. Animals do have legs, after all. They travel (sometimes long distances) in search of food, mates, and spaces to live where human woodland destruction hasn't manifested yet. While you're unlikely to see a big cat on a beach outside of Florida (and even there it isn't common), it would be irresponsible to not mention your need to be prepared for a dangerous wildlife encounter. Beachcombers regularly see foxes and clusters of deer on their beaches. It's very important to realize that if you do encounter these animals at night, the darkness is going to reduce your reaction time if you need to get away, and most forms of wildlife have the capability of seeing a lot better than you do at night. Mating season can also make any animal more aggressive and thus more likely to make unusual moves (especially if they are in a pack). Having knowledge about the species that are known to exist and those that might exist in your area will help you stay safe. The question of whether shell hunters should be armed on the beach is a controversial one that won't be tackled here. If you're interested in nonlethal means, several wildlife experts recommend packing bear spray to protect yourself while you're hunting at night.

Many beaches have human predators, and even beaches you consider safe can change quickly. Within the past few years, a handful of beaches in South Carolina that many shellers have hunted with confidence for decades have become incredibly unsafe. It's no longer advisable to go there before daylight, after the sun sets, or without a partner. For one of those beaches, the

Fun fact: The eyes from a herd of approaching beach deer glow in the light of a headlamp like zombies out of one of those movies your parents told you not to watch before bed. It's good to have a night hunting buddy with you just in case you scare easily.

downfall really happened over a six-month time frame, which is alarmingly fast. Please monitor the crime in your favorite beach locations regularly, and always be aware of your surroundings. Never leave your beach bags unattended if they contain any valuables. Even the shoes you leave behind at your camp might be the target of thieves. Obviously, the risks of being the victim of a crime go up exponentially after dark. You might be surprised to know that there are many people who walk on the beach at night *with no flashlight*. They come out of nowhere. You can't see them until they're right there with you. If those people had designs to hurt you, you would be at a grave disadvantage in the encounter. You should also be aware of the number of anglers and partygoers who spend the night on the beach consuming alcohol or drugs. People under the influence make bad decisions, and being near them when they're in that condition puts you at risk. Exercise your very best judgment when you're out there.

You must keep your phone with you at all times on the beach. Yes, it might get sandy. Of course it might get wet, even if you buy a waterproof case for it. But if you ever need it, you'll regret leaving it behind. If you're night hunting, remember that if something happens to you out there, nobody will know you're in distress. Your phone will be your only lifeline. Use the location share feature on your smartphone so your loved ones will always know where you are.

Before you launch out on a beach and get too far away from your car or lodging, be sure you observe landmarks that will help you find your way back (even in the dark). Don't rely on lights on a specific house or condominium as your guidepost because people tend to turn those off once they go to bed. One of the biggest risks of night hunting is disorientation. It happens to even experienced hunters. Almost all beach access points in every state have abysmal signage. They're small, not reflective to a flashlight, or too similar to one another. It's smart to take a picture of the access point sign before you head out for your walk, and always be aware of the name of the street that runs parallel to the beach, which block you are parked in, and which block you are near as you move. There are also many beaches with extremely limited beach access. In Marco Island, Florida, for instance, all of the big oceanfront resorts block off their entire properties with fencing, and only guests or residents with key access can get off the beach. From the jetties at South Marco, you can walk about a mile and find only two or three places for the public to enter or leave the beach—and none of them are easy to distinguish. Less developed beaches can be just as challenging because all of the houses look the same, and there aren't any lighted piers or brightly colored high rises to serve as discernable landmarks.

Be aware of the potential for fog or cloud cover if you're going night hunting because those factors can contribute greatly to your risk of beach disorientation. If fog or the clouds cover the moon, your major source of light (and the provider of your spatial orientation with the horizon) will be lost.

The dangers of harsh beach landscapes should be respected. It's possible for you to hunt beaches in America that are so remote that you'll walk out of a cell phone signal. In a place like Cape San Blas, Florida, you can travel ten miles up a completely undeveloped beach. You might not see another soul on that hike. The longer you walk during the day, the more the temperature will rise and your need for water will increase. You might get tired and not be able to find shade. You could be hunting a stretch of beach that's not regularly patrolled by lifeguards or park rangers, and if you wind up in need, it might be a long time before you're discovered. It's important to always know the risks of the beach you're hunting and to go prepared. Don't walk until you're completely spent because you have to walk an equal distance back to your car carrying shells. Take twice as much water as you anticipate you'll need.

You can't be in the water more than knee deep in the dark—ever. Too much can go wrong. If there are sharks, you'll never see them coming. As well, being in the water at night when a bite takes place will turn a dicey situation into a life-threatening one. Because of the nighttime water restriction, you also should never wade out to sandbars no matter how tempting it might be. At least some daylight is required before embarking on that expedition. Beyond the fact that wading out to a sandbar puts you too far away from shore in the dark, you have no idea what the currents are doing on any given day until you try them out, and sandbars are notorious for making currents do odd things. You don't want to get out near the sandbar and realize you're in trouble with the current. Additionally, without daylight, it's easy to lose track of what the tide is doing because you're so engrossed with shelling. If you don't recognize that the tide is coming back in, the shallow water you waded through to get out to the sandbar could be over your head on the way back.

If you're hunting on a recently renourished beach where new sand has been pumped in to combat erosion, be aware of the sink hole risk. When a beach is modified in any way and large earth-moving equipment is involved, the stability of the sand is altered. Air pockets can form underneath what looks like solid sand, and you'll not know that until you're knee deep in a hole. When you hit one, you go straight down. Sink holes are a lot worse in

The wonder of T. H. Stone Memorial St. Joseph Peninsula State Park in Cape San Blas, Florida, is that it's so wild and undeveloped. The danger of the park is that it's so wild and undeveloped. It's just you and the dunes out there. The last time I visited, park officials were conducting a manhunt for a missing beachcomber who had to spend the night exposed to the elements without having planned on it. Thankfully, that story had a happy ending, but it reminded me of the need to fully respect treacherous natural landscapes.

the days and weeks after renourishment. Rain also makes them more unstable, particularly if you're hunting while the precipitation is falling.

Watch out for stinging animals like the Portuguese man o' war, which looks like a blue balloon. If you observe one floating in the water, get out immediately because their tentacles can sting you from a distance of many feet. The pain from such encounters is intense. Some unfortunate victims have reported that the sting hurts worse than unmedicated childbirth. Sometimes the small ones don't have that prominent blue color, so they just look like tiny clear balloons. This is why you always need to wear shoes when you're hunting among seaweed, and never walk into seaweed so deep that your feet sink. Sometimes state park rangers post flags warning visitors of the presence of dangerous marine life. Those flags are usually purple, but don't rely on them because there could be a man o' war on the beach on green-flag days. It's impossible for the rangers to detect all of the hazards during their short recognizance walks. Yet despite their danger, the man o' war is among the most alluring animals in the ocean. Take the opportunity to study one if you ever come across it. Just don't touch, and make sure there are no incoming waves that might move it toward you unexpectedly.

There are other animals on the beach that might also sting you, like jellyfish and octopuses. Jellyfish tend to mind their own business. By the time they make it to shore, they're probably in the process of dying because they need oxygen from the ocean water. Octopuses, on the other hand, are a different slimy story. They're cunning. Don't turn your back.

This is why you can't be a distracted beachcomber. You have to pay attention to every step.

Little octopuses like this one have the ability to climb way up into empty seashells, and they wait until much later to pop out and say "ta dah" in your shell bucket. This guy was harmless, and I got him off of my shoe and back into the water without a kerfuffle. The bigger octopuses give me pause. I once had a gigantic octopus encounter on the beach at 4:15 in the morning. It was the first octopus I'd ever met personally, but I knew right away I didn't like him. He was as big as my cat and was pulsating. I also knew that he would die if I left him there because it was freezing. We had a talk, and I explained that I was going to help him, but if he wrapped his slimy arms around me and squeezed like a boa constrictor, I was going to expire right there on the beach. With the ground rules established, I picked him up bare-handed and put him back in the ocean without incident. Helping him was the right thing to do, but it was distressing for us both.

Monitoring Weather Conditions

One of the best parts of being on the beach frequently is seeing some of the most awe-inspiring meteorological displays Mother Nature can conjure. The flip side is that sometimes shellers can get so engaged with what they're finding that they don't notice the first signs that the weather is changing. On any coast, the weather can take a turn with little or no notice. Some of the wildest swings from calm to dangerous weather come in Florida. Sometimes beachcombers get only one subtle hint that things up top are changing—like an unexpected cool breeze—before lightning starts popping, thunder begins to roll, and the bottom drops out. Beaches are an especially dangerous place for humans to be during a surprise storm due to the number of beach umbrellas on any given day. When the straight-line winds blow, the umbrellas can start rolling down the beach. Lightning and the threat of being struck by flying debris are really the top two concerns for beachgoers in a storm situation. As hunters, we have to be even more cautious with the weather than most people. Night hunting removes our ability to interpret the visual cues that the environment sends when it's about to shift gears, so it's all the more important that we study the weather before we go out and review conditions regularly by checking radar while we're in the field. We also must be mindful of how far we have walked away from our beach access point to ensure that we have enough time to walk back in case we need shelter from a pop-up thunderboomer.

Ethical Beachcombing and Why We Don't "Live Shell"

If we want our children and grandchildren to inherit a planet with all of the wonders we have enjoyed, it's our responsibility to model ethical beachcombing for them. This is a loaded concept that often brings out strong emotions and divergent opinions, but it's a conversation that must be had.

Live shelling describes taking from the beach a creature that's still alive. An animal should never die just for the sake of a souvenir. Killing a deer just because its antlers will look nice hanging over your fireplace is a coward's game. Killing a deer for food is a completely different scenario. There are people who harvest live shells (with the proper permits) to eat them. It's really no different than you ordering conch chowder while you're in a restaurant in the Florida Keys. There are some people who will actually pick up live scallops off the beach and eat them right there. While that might be gag-inducing to some, many foodies insist scallops actually taste better fresh and uncooked. There are also people who collect certain edible species of jellyfish off the beach for the purposes of consumption. Choosing to eat seafood is a personal decision, and we should all respect those who do and those who don't.

Where most people diverge from the live shellers is when they are taking those animals simply because they want the shell for decoration or the seahorse or starfish for crafting. This is the wrong choice, and it's a disgusting thing to see.

Some new shellers really don't know how to tell if something they find is alive or dead, and even experienced beachcombers get tricked sometimes. With a seashell, you always want to check the aperture to see if there's a critter in there. Sometimes the animal will look like a blob, and other times it will be a crab with legs. Inevitably, though, even the most careful shellers will accidentally bring an occupied shell home from the beach. Always check your shells thoroughly before you leave the coast to head inland because once you get home, that animal will sadly die, despite your best efforts. It happens to the best of us. Especially when a miniscule crab decides to move into a shell that's too big for it, it can climb so far back in there that you truly can't see it. If possible, let your bucket rest on the sand for twenty minutes before you go home to see if anything unexpected starts moving in there.

Many of the big shells that you see in water (aperture side down) are occupied. If you go to pick them up and there is any resistance, that means that the animal is inside, and it's partially down in the sand. Let go, and don't disturb it.

The horse conch on the left is clearly occupied by an animal. You can see it in the aperture or hole. Even though it might move slowly like a snail, you can usually observe the animal's movement. The shell on the right is empty. The aperture is hollow, and you can peer down into the opening. If you pick up an occupied shell but you are 100 percent confident the animal is dead, it's still best to leave it on the beach because you'll have a booger of a time getting the stink out.

Sand dollars are less tricky when it comes to determining if they're alive or dead. Live sand dollars are covered in hair called cilia, which looks like fur. If you pick up a sand dollar that is hairy (particularly if it's dark colored, with a purple or even burgundy tint), it's alive. You can often see the cilia moving, and sometimes you can even observe sand dollars scooting on the beach. If you find a sand dollar with no fur at all, it's dead. Occasionally, you'll discover one that has some fur but is mostly slick. If ever in doubt, leave them behind.

Starfish are a much more complicated story. A live starfish can have such subtle movements that they're risky to take home. It really is best if you don't touch them at all. If, however, you know that a beachcomber coming behind you is collecting live ones, by all means get out ahead and put all of them back in the ocean.

It's very tempting to pick up wildlife because it provides a super opportunity for a photograph, and holding unusual animals is a thrill. Most experienced shellers who have been on the scene for a long time eventually come to the point where they handle animals only if they're troubled and need help. Our positions and perspectives should change as we mature and learn.

This sand dollar is clearly alive. It's covered in hair and on the move, as evidenced by the trail in the sand and the conglomeration of sand on its front hood. Also notice the deep purple color that's often seen with the live animals. This sand dollar should be left to his own devices.

These sand dollars are 100 percent dead. They no longer have any fur, so they can be taken from the beach. Many times the already expired sand dollar will be white, light gray, or tan.

Even the shellers with the best intentions make mistakes sometimes and accidentally bring a live creature home. When it happens, it's enough to be sorry and say it out loud to the ocean. The difference is when you know and you take live shells anyway. Also recognize that most shelled creatures can survive on the beach in the few hours it takes for the tide to come back in, and most have the capability of moving themselves back toward the water if they wish.

Aside from avoiding live shelling, ethical beachcombing also has a lot of other facets. If you're hunting a beach that has nesting turtles, you need to use a red light instead of white flashlights and headlamps during nesting season, which usually runs from April to October. Turtles need the white light of the moon to help them navigate for nesting activities, so our white lights interfere with that. Even in areas that aren't quite as strict about their light rules, it's good to do the right thing

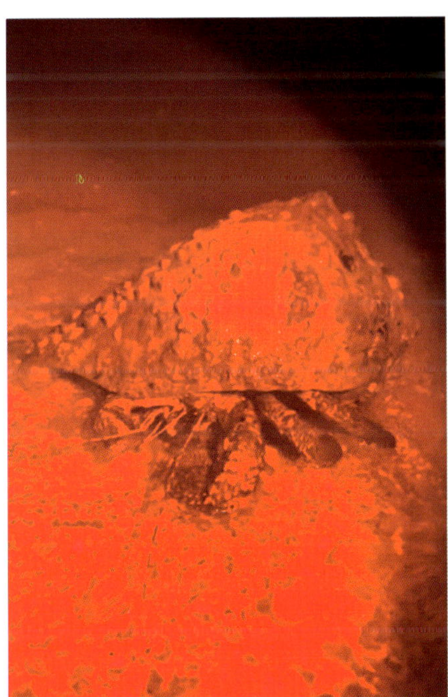

This mammoth Sanibel whelk shell was inhabited by a very discontented crab. It's hard to tell from the picture, but he was as big as a football and not in the mood to play games. Using a red light is a serious challenge because it makes it harder for a sheller to see at night. You can learn to adjust your eyes to it with practice though.

on your own. If you come upon injured wildlife on the beach (or if you see someone harassing wildlife), please call local wildlife or law enforcement officials when the situation warrants.

Responsible beachcombers should also leave the beach in better shape than they found it. This means picking up other people's trash, especially hazardous trash that could injure someone else (like discarded fishing tackle with rusty hooks or broken glass shards). If you're going to use recycled plastic grocery bags or resealable kitchen bags to collect shells, be mindful that the wind can easily blow them out of your hands. And for the love of all that is holy, please stop releasing balloons in memory of deceased loved ones. They end up on the beach—not in heaven.

Once you get really deep into this hobby, you'll walk the shore all the time in contexts where your behavior is not monitored by others. Ethical beachcombing isn't about what you do when other people are looking; it's about the choices you make when nobody is around. Do right by the ocean because those honorable decisions matter.

Recently I was on a paid shelling excursion and wound up on a boat with a family from another state. On the way out, the captain gave us the talk about not collecting any live creatures because he knew he was taking us to an island at an extra-low tide when there would be many occupied shells on the beach. Of course, when we arrived, I flew off the boat like I had jet propulsion and didn't come back until the very last second before the boat left. When I returned, though, I noticed a huge bucket of whelks—all very clearly alive. There was no way any person could look at those shells and think they were dead. Let's just say I made a good old-fashioned scene, and I'm not sorry. If the animal is alive and you know it, it has to stay at the beach, especially if you're on my boat.

Essential Gear

It's a common dilemma for a beachcomber to be torn between wanting to be really prepared on the beach with gear but then also not wanting to carry a bunch of gadgets and gizmos. You'll definitely regret carrying the things you never actually needed, so below is a curated list of some of the essential gear, along with some specific recommendations for reliable, user-friendly products.

Flashlights and Headlamps

Even if you aren't going to be a night hunter, you may still arrive to the beach slightly before sunrise and need a flashlight. You might also get on a hot streak with a tide as the sun is setting and need a flashlight unexpectedly because you aren't ready to stop searching. It's in your best interest long term to buy lighting devices that are rechargeable instead of fooling with batteries. Most of the high-lumen models of 50,000 or 90,000 are nothing but a gimmick. While they might shine insanely bright for ten minutes, they tend to start dimming more quickly than the lower-lumen models that provide steady light. Kobalt, Hyper Tough, and DanForce make dependable rechargeable flashlights and headlamps in the 500- to 1,000-lumen ranges that you can trust. You should also consider getting a model that has the capacity to switch from white light to red light in case you do some hunting in a turtle nesting area. Reading the customer reviews is imperative because people are honest about the equipment that doesn't hold its charge. There's nothing worse than getting an hour into your hunt two miles away from your car and realizing your lights are fizzling out. As well, with headlamps, the long-term comfort of the head strap really matters. Wearing a ball cap underneath them helps. The weight of the battery packs on some headlamp models can also give you a massive headache over time. Test all of these factors when you get new lights to ensure you're making a good investment in something that will serve you well for a long time.

Footwear

Sometimes wearing shoes on the beach is necessary, but try as much as possible to walk barefoot because it's so valuable for your health. We all know that being near the ocean benefits the human body. Scientific studies have

You won't convince me otherwise: Kino's Lily sandals are the most functional shoe ever created. They're inexpensive, machine-washable, durable, comfortable, and adorable. After a few months of continuous surf hunting, the soles will begin to curl. But their retail price is so cheap that you can afford to replace them. I regularly walk ten miles a day in them and never miss a beat. Get your pair at the store on Fitzpatrick Street in Key West or online, but remember, only the Lily style will do for shelling.

proven it over and over. Our brains respond positively to the sound and rhythm of the waves. The fresh air is beneficial for our lungs. The vitamin D and the warmth from the sun make us happy. Barefoot walking will make you feel better, help you sleep better, and reduce your aches, pains, headaches, and stress. The phenomenon is called grounding, and it's a real thing. Even a little bit of time spent outside barefoot in the grass, on the dirt, or over sand can have instant and dramatic impacts on health. Walking without shoes will also toughen up the soles of the feet, so walking over shells won't hurt. There are beach contexts where wearing shoes is imperative to prevent injury, though. In that case, go with flip-flops from Kino (the Lily style), which is manufactured by a family in Key West. The only drawback to them is that they need a little rinse every hour or so while you're beachcombing to ensure no sand has gotten under the leather strap. A lot of shellers really love the FITKICKS water socks for a more full-coverage water shoe. However, a full-coverage shoe is going to give you that unfortunate water squish when you walk, and you'll wind up with a wicked farmer's tan on your feet.

Barefoot shoes are the best shoes for shelling.

Boots/Waders

Waders and knee-high boots can be really helpful when the ocean temperature dips and you can't stand the cold. Waders are also ideal for people who get so into hunting that they don't pay attention to big waves coming up from behind. You always want to go with a lightweight wader. As you're testing options in the store, pick them up and think about what kind of weight you want hanging on your body. Look for designs with water socks at the bottom so you can wear a slide flip-flop or boot over them. Remember as well to size up your waders in case you want to add extra layers of clothes for really cold days or in the event that you hit the cupcakes a little too hard.

Buckets

Choose cheaper buckets—like Dollar Tree cheaper. Admittedly, they aren't without their flaws. The handles are really their weakness. They'll eventually rust, and the wire handles will start popping out. But that happens long after you've gotten your money's worth out of them. The best thing Dollar Tree buckets have going for them is they're lightweight. The nicer buckets that will last longer are so heavy, and when you add shells they're just too much. Keep a small piece of Tupperware in the top of the bucket for shark teeth or the more delicate shells you find.

Mesh Shelling Bags

Mesh bags with cross-body straps are super-duper handy when you want to go hands-free on your walk. They also fold up to nothing in a pocket, so you can carry a spare in case the shelling action just explodes on you. One drawback to the mesh shelling bag is that it will cause sand to sprinkle down your leg all day if you don't thoroughly rinse your shells before putting them inside.

Hats

Shells and shark teeth are easier to see when your face is shaded, especially if you're walking into the sun or at times of the day when the sun is directly overhead. Interestingly, it's also easier to see seashells and shark teeth with the naked eye, so sunglasses can actually interfere with your vision. Your best choice for headwear is a ball cap because it gets the shade job done with the bill in the front, and you can turn it around backward if you're hunting during a time when shade isn't needed. Either way it also keeps your hair from blowing in your face. While wide-brimmed sun hats provide a lot of shade coverage, they're also more likely to get caught by the wind, and you don't want to spend half your day running down the beach chasing them.

Backpacks

If you're going on a shelling or fossil excursion or if you know you're going to be walking long distances, wear at least a little drawstring backpack to hold your car keys, your phone, a bottle of water, a snack, sunscreen, bug spray, a poncho, and any essential medications.

Snorkel Gear

If you plan to do any snorkeling for shells, it's really prudent to invest in durable gear designed to last. You can waste a wad of money buying swimming-pool-grade goggles that barely make it through a summer. Instead, visit a dive shop and get some recommendations for top-quality gear. Some shops (like Divers Direct in the Keys) even have prescription-strength goggles for bespectacled shellers.

Optional: Scoopers, Rakes, and Sifters

You either love or hate these tools. If you love them, read the reviews and invest in high-quality products known for their durability. If you select models that are made of metal, be sure to rinse them with fresh water after each use to prevent the salt water from corroding them prematurely. Those who dig extra gadgets might also consider purchasing an underwater viewing bucket, which is essentially a five-gallon bucket with a see-through bottom that allows you to get a clear look at the ocean floor if you're knee or thigh deep in the water. They're an undeniable pain in the bum to carry around (as are all scoopers, rakes, and sifters), but if that doesn't bother you, go for it.

Before you leave for a beachcombing adventure, fully analyze the situation you'll be facing on that specific beach. How far will you walk? How long will you be gone? What does the weather forecast say? It can take some time (and some lessons learned the hard way) to discern what you should and should not take. Getting the proper balance in the gear you select is crucial to a successful hunt, so keep experimenting.

Cleaning and Displaying Your Shells

If you have spent any time in an online seashell forum, you know how contentious the debate about cleaning seashells and fossils can be. Not only are there arguments about whether the shell should be cleaned or left in its original state, shell collectors argue about the best methods for removing unwanted sediments and barnacles and for shining and polishing. While opinions abound and the results vary, the advice offered here is designed to give you the best potential outcome with the least amount of risk if you do decide to process your beach finds in some way.

Before you make any decisions, you have to first consider what you ultimately want to do with your shells. If there's any chance you might eventually want to sell them or pass them on to a child or grandchild who might one day sell them, you'll be glad you kept your shells in the most natural state possible. There are some collectors who will not buy a restored or polished shark tooth, a bleached sand dollar, or an acid-dipped, lacquered, or polished seashell. By making irrevocable changes to your shells, you might be cutting out a huge percentage of your future buyer pool.

You want to employ the least toxic, least expensive, least labor-intensive, and least extreme cleaning method first. If you're unhappy with the results, you can move on to the next method.

Rain Water

It sounds way too easy, but you'll be flabbergasted at what rainwater can do to clean up both shells and fossils. In some cases, a few weeks outside will get your beach finds clean as a whistle. Rainwater is a particularly effective method for cleaning sea biscuits. Depending on how much rain you get, a few months in the elements can leave your sea biscuits with the prettiest bright white color, with all of the clumps of brown sediment washed away. Rainwater can also take care of the odor from some stinky shells. In many instances, you don't have to scrub or soak, and none of your beach finds will ever be in danger of being damaged by the process. The dripping action of the water over many rain storms does the work for you. It doesn't get any

The biscuits on the bottom row are fresh from the beach. Those on the top row were left out in the rain for a month. Over time, rain water will wash away the brown sediment clumps (like the one on the bottom row in the middle) and the gray/black patina from the surface. Depending on how much rain you get, usually a few weeks will do the trick, and the rain will not diminish the color of the floral design on the top.

easier, safer, cheaper, or less risky than that. Be advised that if you brought something putrid home from the beach, wild animals might be attracted by the odor and carry it away in the night, so put it somewhere safe. Racoons are notorious for sniffing out smelly shells and skittering away with them.

Apple Cider Vinegar Soak

If you have fossils (like shark teeth) with sediments or encrustations you would like to remove, try a soak in pure apple cider vinegar (no water dilution), followed by a careful scrub with a wire brush and a thorough rinse with fresh water. This is the preferred method of many dealers who take fossils from the ocean floor that then need to be cleaned before sale. Vinegar is also safe to have around the house, easy to find, and inexpensive, and no special disposal methods are needed for the refuse. Even though vinegar is nontoxic, it can sting your skin, so wear rubber gloves when you work with it. Two warnings here, though. If you leave a fossil in an apple cider vinegar soak for too long, you might "burn" the exterior. That burning will make the enamel of the tooth look permanently cloudy and dull, which will diminish its value. If you're using the vinegar soaking technique, be sure to check on your fossils each hour for progress. Second, *you should NEVER put a seashell in any kind of vinegar.* Because seashells are made mostly of calcium carbonate, the acid in the vinegar will break down the shell and cause it to disintegrate. Your seashells will go bye-bye in no time in a bucket of any kind of vinegar.

The vast majority of the things you find on the beach only need to be rinsed off to maximize their natural beauty. Rain water works like a champ on pieces like the slipper shell pictured above. There's a little pocket on the back side that looks like a bedroom slipper.

White Vinegar Soak

Many shellers use an undiluted white vinegar soak to clean hard fossils like sea biscuits, and home experiments with this method in the past have yielded moderate success. The soak takes a few hours, and you still wind

This shell is a prime example of periostracum you want to keep. Mother Nature put a perfect stamp on this shell, and altering it in any way would be a horrible shame.

up having to scrub them. If you have collected a really beaten-up sea biscuit, the rain water method is not going to magically put it into the grade-A category. The precipitation will just clean it and brighten the finish. If your biscuits have gnarly clumps of sediment on them, the vinegar soak alone might not get them off either, so you often still have to use a Dremel tool. It's no fun wearing safety glasses and a mask and still having big chunks fly up and hit your face—not to mention the very real possibility that you will Dremel a hole right through your very own hand. As well, the white vinegar soaks often leave behind a white residue that seems to leak out of the biscuit. Additionally, leaving items like sea biscuits in vinegar for too long fades out the floral design on the top, which is where all of the beauty really is. Once you realize how effective and easy the rain water solution is, you'll never soak in vinegar again. Don't forget to rinse your fossils after a white vinegar soak just as you would with an apple cider vinegar bath.

Bleach Soak

If the rain water has not sufficiently cleaned your shells, the next method to try is a bleach soak. You'll find different recipes for how to bleach soak your shells online, but considering that it's better to be more cautious with your processes, you should always start by diluting unscented bleach with water in a one-to-one ratio and leave shells soaking for a very short time, checking progress hourly. There are some brave souls who put their shells in pure bleach for a month at a time, but that requires some serious nerve. Bleach soaking is very effective if you've brought home a smelly shell, particularly those that have been collected during a red tide. In that instance, you want to kill any bacteria that hitchhiked home.

Often when horse conchs are found, they're covered with sharp barnacles and have a flaky brown layer on the outside called periostracum that can add to the beauty of the shell. Other times you can tell from the colors of the aperture that the cleaned shell would have a tremendous vibrance. The choice is yours, but don't be surprised if you find yourself fighting with your own sentimentality. There's a lot to be said for keeping shells in the same condition that Mother Nature offered them.

A one-to-one bleach/water soak of even an hour will often be enough to make the barnacles of a shell pop off easily with a dental tool, and some if not all of the periostracum might be loosened enough to remove with an old toothbrush. If not, just put the shell (completely submerged) back in the bucket and check again in an hour. Some stubborn horse conchs may need a

The trio of photographs above shows the transformation that a quick diluted bleach soak can deliver. This progression took approximately an hour.

few days in a bleach soak. When that happens, always remove the shell from the solution overnight because you won't be awake to monitor it. Once the shell has been processed to your satisfaction, rinse it well with water before you touch it with your bare hands. It's advisable to wear rubber gloves to avoid irritating your skin with the bleach. As well, when you're submerging your shells and moving them back and forth from the soaking bucket, be careful not to splash because bleach can damage your eyes and skin and stain your clothes. When shells with big apertures are submerged, the water rushes with more force than you might expect, and splash-back is common.

Mineral Oil

Many shellers love using a napkin to rub a small amount of mineral oil on their shells to pump up the color. The effect might be temporary, so you may need to repeatedly treat them. Before applying the oil, the shell needs to be completely dry, and then afterward the oil needs a day to dry fully. You should be aware that mineral oil can have nasty ingredients that aren't great for your skin, but oiling is a ton safer than acid dipping if you really want to improve the appearance of your shells.

Muriatic Acid Dips

Using muriatic acid for any fossil/seashell cleaning is a terrible idea. It's incredibly dangerous to use. Read the label—if it splashes on your skin or in your eyes, you'll be headed to an emergency room. It's toxic to even breathe the fumes. You have to work with it outdoors, and you can still be negatively affected by the odor. Muriatic acid is a risky thing to even have stored around your house if you have children or pets. If it spills, you've got a big problem on your hands. You also can't just pour it down the drain or into the yard when you're finished using it. It's hazardous waste that has to be disposed of per regulations. If you leave your shells in an acid dip for even a few seconds too long, they'll be ruined forever. Muriatic acid dips pose way too many risks, especially considering that less harsh, less expensive, and less dangerous methods do the same work. Many fellow shellers "dip" and love it. Most of them are crafters who sell their creations, so having really vibrant seashell colors matters to them. If you're going to acid dip, remember that you should

No shiny shell should ever be dipped in muriatic acid. These would include (from left to right) olives, gaudy nauticas, and junonias. Leave them just as they are or your sorrow will run deep.

never process a naturally glossy shell (like a cowrie or olive). The acid will destroy the shine irreparably.

Display

Every beachcomber is curious about how other folks display their beloved ocean finds. Once you have amassed a collection of any size, you'll want a way to protect, organize, and show off your favorite fossils and seashells. Plastic specimen trays are a handy display option. They come in a variety of sizes and configurations, and they're stackable, which is a useful feature. The only drawback is they do scratch easily, so a little bit of tissue paper layered between the boxes is needed. BoxBox is an outstanding brand (look for the red sticker on the side). As you are filling your cases, remember that less is really more. You want guests who visit your house to actually see the highlights, not necessarily the whole collection. These boxes also make it much easier for you to know what you have and where it's all located if you're still working on species identification. The crafty shellers go wild with shadow boxes and displays in glass-top tables. If using a glue gun to cover your entire fireplace with seashells makes you happy, by all means go for it, friend. But you can get a whole lot of satisfaction from simple stackable trays to showcase your finds.

The Stinky Red Tide

Red tide, which is an algae bloom that takes over an ecosystem, is bad news all the way around for shellers. Its presence might close beaches. When it hits, the idyllic coastline where you find your seashells and your happiness might be littered with rotting dead fish killed by the release of the algae's toxins. The shells you do manage to collect will stink to high heaven. You won't be able to get in the water due to the risk of skin infection, and it might irritate your respiratory system and cause a hacking cough. The wind direction controls how bad the respiratory irritation might be, so always carry a paper mask just in case the wind shifts when red tide might be present.

Red tides have become pretty frequent in Florida, and they sometimes last for months. However, the bad impacts of the red tide wax and wane constantly. You can follow a bloom's progress daily on the Florida Fish and Wildlife Conservation Commission website. New updates are added each day by 5:00 p.m. These results are gathered from both water quality testing and aerial views of the water; you can actually see the algae bloom from the air when it's really bad. If red tide is looming around the time of your vacation and your enjoyment of the trip would be hindered by not being able to get in the water, then you might want to consider an alternative plan.

Our family hunts during red tides all the time in Florida, but we do avoid the water when conditions are deemed dangerous by local officials. We wear waders and boots to prevent the water from contacting our skin, and any body part that touches the water is treated with hand sanitizer. I've seen pictures of shellers who have had small cuts or even jellyfish stings get infected by the red tide, and the results can be horrific.

Avoiding "No-See-Ums," Chiggers, and Other Devious Bugs

There are few things more miserable in this world than taking a boat to a barrier island, being unexpectedly swarmed by biting insects, and having no access to bug spray or itch relief. It's a mystery how the early global explorers stood it. You can't get away from the swarm, and you can't ignore the discomfort and keep going. Your shelling bag should always include multiple forms of bug spray and itch-relief lotion. You just never know what species is going to be biting wherever you're going, and every individual's body chemistry causes the bugs to respond differently. One person in your search party might be eaten alive, while others might be relatively unaffected. One bug spray might work one day, but the next day it might fail. Therefore, having options and first aid remedies is essential.

There are many kinds of bugs that might try to ruin your day while you're shelling. The biting midge is more commonly referred to as the no-see-um because the critters are so small you're likely not going to see them doing their dirty work. Coastal Georgia and Florida are notorious for no-see-ums.

The best times to shell and see wildlife seem to always coincide with the worst times to be assaulted by vexatious beach bugs. It pays to spray.

They like the time right around sunup and sundown, and usually after the sun is completely up their nuisance fades. They're attracted to white clothing and exposed skin, so wearing darker colors and clothes with long sleeves and pant legs will help your cause. All bugs including no-see-ums are drawn to light, so they will mob your face if you're using a headlamp. You can get hundreds of no-see-um bites before you realize it because you won't feel the impact, and the itch tends to come on like a slow burn. Their sneak attack is the main reason you need to apply multiple forms of protection preemptively instead of waiting to see if they're out that day. Always assume they will be. Once the itch hits, it's intense, and those little bites will plague you for days. The more you scratch, the worse they become. Baths and showers can also reignite no-see-um bites that you thought had run their course.

Chiggers are another pest that can wreck your outings. Chiggers can get you anywhere, but they love marshes and anywhere with brush. Whereas no-see-ums like exposed skin, chiggers prefer to root into the tight parts of your clothes (like the waist of your pants or beneath the elastic of your undies or bra). These are the most inconvenient places to have an uncontrollable itch. The aftermath of a chigger attack is even worse than that from no-see-ums because the chiggers hang onto you and keep eating your skin. The southern home remedy is to put fingernail polish over the bites to smother the bugs. Nearly every southern kid has gone to church with his Mamaw's rose-colored fingernail polish all over his chigger bites at one point or another. The polish strategy works, but you don't want to get to that step in the process. Protect yourself and avoid the bites altogether.

Beachcombers also need to be aware of good old-fashioned mosquitos and God-awful biting flies. Both can demolish your day if you forgot to pack the spray.

If you can, tend toward more natural options with your bug sprays. It's always best to try the safest and least toxic option first. Your first line of defense is an array of essential oils: citronella, lemongrass, rosemary, thyme, lemon eucalyptus, eucalyptus, and peppermint for deterrence and lavender for itch in the event of a bite. The next tool in your arsenal will be a botanical blend like the line of No Natz products. They even have bug-deterrent candles that really work.

If you're going to be on an island for camping or on a boat tour where you can't control how long you'll be out or if you'll have access to shelter, don't forget to take at minimum three kinds of bug spray and have some anti-itch cream and at least one dose of antihistamine for each person in your group with you. It can't be overstated how much agony you could potentially be in if you don't prepare adequately.

I'll not allow no-see-ums to take over my favorite sunrises. The bug-fighting arsenal in my shelling backpack makes them tremble in their deceitful little boots. Not me. Not today.

Wedding Shells

Wedding shells are nonnative species (often from Indonesia) that are purchased in gift shops for a cheap price and then dropped on the beach by a flower girl or scattered around in a ring on the ground for a wedding ceremony. They tend to pop up on beaches where people tie the knot, but they can also be transplanted from their original location for a lot of other reasons. Sometimes people will purchase shells to sprinkle on the beach for their children to find, and not all of them get recovered. It's also possible for nonnative species to make it back to a beach after a hurricane destroys a community where a lot of shellers had private collections in their homes. This was especially true after Hurricane Ian decimated Sanibel Island, Florida, in 2022.

I found this odd shell last year at one of my favorite honey holes in Key West, Florida, and was totally puzzled because I'd never seen one before in that area. With a little bit of research and some help from very knowledgeable friends, I discovered that it was a volute shell native to the Pacific, not the Atlantic. After making a dorky joke about it being in the Conch Republic on vacation, I realized that it's what is known as a "wedding shell."

So here's an idea. Instead of jumping down the throat of a fellow sheller who you suspect is posting online pictures of a "fake shell" he or she bought in a beach shop to make it look like a great discovery, how about taking a deep breath and backing away from the keyboard. I recently had an extended conversation with a well-known fossil hunter about this very subject. He admitted that there have been several of his discoveries in the past few years that he would have never believed had he not been the one to actually find those things in those locations. Just because you've never picked up a particular shell like the one in the picture on a beach doesn't mean it's impossible to find that shell on that beach.

Sometimes in seashell forums things can get spicy when a person posts a picture of what he or she found on a particular beach and then is accused of intentionally faking the event for the sake of a photo opportunity. The likelihood is that the shell was found by someone honest who just didn't realize he or she was collecting a piece left over from a wedding. Don't ever be disappointed when you come upon a wedding shell—you did find it, after all. It was just on holiday very far away from home.

Albino Shells

Albino seashells are among the most unique things you'll come across on a beach. Most experienced shellers have found only a few, so they're seriously rare. Albino simply means that the shell lacks pigmentation. So instead of the expected Florida fighting conch with varied designs in brown or even purple hues, what you get with an albino Florida fighting conch (like those pictured here) is a gorgeous pure white shell. Because of their exquisite beauty, albino seashells are sold for very inflated prices on the retail market. Don't ever sell the ones you find. Note that an albino shell is different from a sun-bleached shell. Even with sun-bleached shells, you can usually use a black light and see the remnants of the original color design. Albino shells aren't faded or bleached—they never had color.

The albino tulip shell in the center was found in Kice Island, Florida. The two albino Florida fighting conchs were picked up on Marco Island, Florida. The corridor between Sanibel and the Ten Thousand Islands is where many albino shells are found. I'll never part with any of mine for any amount of money.

Appreciating "Mini" Shells

The cool kids who use shelling lingo have named the small shells that rarely get noticed minis. While they aren't as dramatic as a massive whelk or horse conch, there's still so much charm in them to appreciate. You're going to want to make friends with other people who recognize the value of the smaller shells because they see the world through a very intuitive and thoughtful lens. Collectors whose perceptions are scaled up only to the premium shells that everyone else desires are missing a big part of the beachcombing journey. Your experience will be so much richer when you pause to really feel the energy the micros put off too.

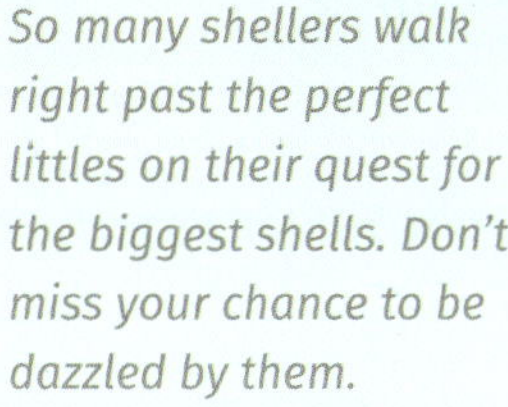

So many shellers walk right past the perfect littles on their quest for the biggest shells. Don't miss your chance to be dazzled by them.

The micro-shelling is full throttle for the entire journey down the Florida Keys. When you're stuck in traffic on the A1A, pull over and find a beach on the Atlantic side. You'll end up with a handful of joy like the picture above in no time.

Looking Up for Sunrises and Sunsets

As a beachcomber who gets totally consumed in the hunt, it's easy to forget to look up and appreciate the beauty that's all around you. Really intent shellers often get more focused on the products of the hunt and can thus become less in tune with the experience. Sunrises and sunsets are some of Mother Nature's best gifts, and it would be a shame to miss them because our eyes are trained on the sand. We all need to be more intentional about pausing and letting the details of our natural environment really sink in to our souls. The Florida Keys are known as the best place in the United States

If I die tomorrow, I want to know today's sunset was enjoyed to the fullest.

to see a sunset. You want to make it over to the Gulf side if you're coming down the Keys in the evening for the best vantage point. Key West is obviously the mecca for a legendary sunset, as the islanders have devoted a whole nightly festival to the activity. The Ten Thousand Islands also deliver a fine nightly spectacle. Wherever you are—no matter the time of day—look up because you just never know what surprises await.

If the world has knocked the wind out of you, a rare red sunrise will bring you back to life. It will allow you to feel the pulse of nature unlike any other experience.

Knowing the Rules and Regulations

Those who regularly go hunting or fishing automatically think about the state and local rules and regulations that govern those activities. Shell and fossil hunters don't always think in those terms, but they should. You should never go and hunt in an area before you have figured out what you are and are not allowed to do. If your hunting is going to take place in a country where you're a visitor, it's even more critical that you do your research. The very last thing you want on your vacation is to end up in jail over contraband seashells. We've all got friends who love us enough to keep bail money handy, but they would probably draw the line at crossing international waters to help us out.

You must know which species are protected and that you are therefore not allowed to harvest without risk of hefty fines and potential jail time. Thankfully, many areas have laws in place that prohibit live shelling without a permit, which you can obtain if you're harvesting for consumption. What you don't want is to have a sneaky critter way up inside of a protected seashell slip past your inspection and get you in legal trouble. There are even some species of turtles in America that you're not allowed to possess even if you find their clearly dead remains on the beach.

If you're going to hunt in a state park, know that many of them have their own rules about what you can harvest alive (like fish) and even what you can take out (like shells). For instance, you can keep the shells found in Fort Zachary Taylor State Park in Key West and Bahia Honda State Park in Big Pine Key, but you can't pocket anything you find in John Pennekamp Coral Reef State Park in Key Largo—all within the state of Florida. And speaking of Florida, you *do not* want to get caught with a live queen conch shell there.

You wouldn't go fishing without getting a permit and following the catch limits. It's wise to take shelling rules and regulations just as seriously.

The offense can be punishable with imprisonment. It is, however, legal to take a queen conch as long as there is no living organism in it and you are not within the boundaries of a park with its own individual collection rules.

As well, the different airlines and cruise lines you utilize may have varied rules about the shells that can and can't be taken on board from your destination. International customs is not the place you want to be having a discussion about why your luggage is loaded with seashells. Before you take anything, research the rules that will apply to the carriers you'll use and all of the countries you'll travel through to get home.

Lastly, if you're hunting on land that's not a public beach, make sure you know who owns it and if you're allowed to be there. Some property owners will press charges because they're understandably tired of people trespassing on their property.

The old adage that it's better to beg for forgiveness than ask for permission doesn't apply here. No seashell is worth prison time.

Whenever you arrive at a beach location, it's wise to read the signage. It pays to be really clear about the rules related to where you can and can't take off your clothes. Just so you're aware, Longboat Key, Florida, is a no.

Resources and Recommended Online Forums

It wasn't very long ago that curious beachcombers who were eager to learn more about shelling had only print resources available, such as a select few books and identification postcards found in beach shops. Within the past decade, though, social media has been used brilliantly to bring shelling and fossil education to a whole new audience on a daily basis. There's still great value to holding a field guide in your hand (like this very book) and having access to it to make your own comparison with a specimen in your hand. Simultaneously, you also now have the capacity to access one of the many excellent Facebook pages dedicated to the hobby to see what everyone else is finding in real time that day.

The best fresh seashell identification books are written by a couple named Dawn and Blair Witherington. They've released numerous terrific beachcombing titles, and nobody will ever produce higher quality guides for seashell identification. You need all of their books in your home library, but it would be smart to begin with *Florida's Living Beaches* because it's so comprehensive. You're also going to want *Florida's Seashells: A Beachcomber's Guide* and *Living Beaches of Georgia and the Carolinas: A Beachcomber's Guide.*

For fossil identification, you don't want to miss Bob, Pam, and Ashby Gale's outstanding *A Beachcomber's Guide to Fossils.* Their text filled a massive gap in the book market, and beachcombers everywhere are so glad they wrote it. My 2015 book *Shark Tooth Hunting*

on the Carolina Coast will provide identification and strategy help for your shark tooth hunt.

Your next most important resource is the website of the Bailey-Matthews National Shell Museum in Sanibel, Florida (https://shellmuseum.org). Once on the main page, click on "Shells & Science" and then "Southwest Florida Shells Guide" to access the museum's fabulous free identification tools. The Bailey-Matthews facility was severely damaged by Hurricane Ian, so any donation you can offer to help their rebuilding efforts would go to a very worthy cause.

Finally, reading the social media forums each day will be an indispensable part of your development as a sheller. These pages give you both the macro and micro perspectives you need to hunt well. The discussion threads allow you to see the bigger picture: *What locations tend to be hot over time? What region should I select for my next shelling vacation?* Concurrently, you'll be able to pick up on details that will allow you to fine-tune your strategy once you arrive: *What location within driving distance of the vacation I'm on is hitting right now? Which beach should I select for a paid excursion based on pictures I've seen from other people who have taken the charters within the past week?* Below is a list of some of the best social media pages you should follow to keep your shelling intellect sharp.

The Shellinators

Perhaps the best national Facebook group dedicated to seashell hunting is the Shellinators. One of the smartest things you can do to expand your education is read every comment every day. This will allow you to learn new species from the repetition of seeing the pictures, and your attention will be drawn to the rare species when you see a poster flipping out and thousands of others liking and commenting. You'll also have the opportunity to interact with people who are more knowledgeable than you so you can absorb what they know over time. Some of the best folks in the seashell identification game watch the group and chime in with correct species names when needed. Be

If you post "What do I have here?" in the Shellinators Facebook group, it will be only a matter of minutes before someone says "Longspine star snail!"

sure to read the rules thoroughly so you aren't muted or banned because you need access to this educational outlet. It's also recommended that you don't post for a while until you get the hang of what is and isn't allowed. Just lay low and read. Once you do start posting, be sure you don't name any specific locations in the Ten Thousand Islands where you might be hunting. Instead, just say something vague like "found in the 10K." The Shellinators page will definitely become one of your favorites in very short order.

Carolina Seashellers

You'll do well to regularly scope out the Carolina Seashellers page. The regional shelling groups on Facebook are fun because they offer a really focused perspective on the species available in a relatively small geographic area. You can increase your identification skills quickly by joining niche social media groups like this one. The only drawback to this page is that crafting posts are allowed. No offense to the crafters out there, but for people who are just interested in beachcombing, the decoupaging can go too far sometimes.

East Coast Fossil Club

East Coast Fossil Club is the most practical and thought-provoking fossil forum. Even though it focuses primarily on fossils (including shark teeth), seashells are also in the mix there because shells can fossilize just like a tooth or bone. As with the Shellinators group, there are some people with next-level

You can post a picture like the one above in the East Coast Fossil Club Facebook group, and there will likely be an expert who can name every single thing in view as soon as you ask for help.

knowledge standing by on East Coast Fossil to provide quick and accurate answers when you've found something puzzling on the beach.

Myrtle Beach Shark Teeth

The Myrtle Beach Shark Teeth page has so much to recommend it beyond just pictures of Horry County, South Carolina, shark teeth. The moderator, Charles Shelton Jr., works really hard to provide educational content like interviews with local experts and video tours of cool ocean-related museums. You'll like it, so join today.

Shell Forum Etiquette

These social media groups work only when everyone behaves, so you have to play nice; nobody wants a meanie in the discussion thread. Beyond being kind, though, there are many expectations of online forum behavior specific to shelling that a newcomer might not recognize. Below are some suggestions for things to avoid to ensure you stay in the good graces of the page moderators and learn as much as possible.

- Avoid over-posting. Limit yourself to one post per day and no more than two or three a week if you're on a cool vacation. Otherwise, you shouldn't be posting daily.
- Don't be the "Where are you?" pest. Posters who want to share their location do so. If their location is not indicated, assume there's a reason. Many experienced hunters intentionally don't share their locations, some for safety reasons, others out of annoyance with people who don't seem interested in doing the trial-and-error work for themselves. Hold your comments, and study the post instead. Very often you can figure out where that person was based on context clues. If you're observant on a daily basis, you can watch patterns develop that tell you where the hot spots are. The expansion of webcam installation at so many piers and resorts now also makes it possible for you to scope out what's happening on beaches many states away. Use that technology to your advantage. While the minute details of the beach won't be in focus, a webcam view can often determine if there's a shell line exposed, how big it is, and where it is on the beach.
- Stay above the fray when disagreements do break out. Don't make the work of the moderators any harder than it already is. Even though you might have strong feelings about the content someone posted, online squabbles rarely change anyone's mind. Hold your tongue so you don't get muted or booted.
- Use the search function in your groups to find answers without having to ask. If you're traveling to a new beach, join the Facebook community page for that area and search "seashells" or "shark teeth." Often you'll see posts like a picture of an incredible seashell and a local captioning it

"Beach Access #5 was fabulous today" or "Look what the shell beds at the lighthouse gave me this morning." You can glean so much information from local experts when you do your detective work. Likewise, use the search function within the seashell and fossil forums to explore the names of beaches you want to visit. Once you have a list of the beach communities that interest you, you can create a map for your trip. This research can save you so much time by helping to identify the areas that you can probably skip.

- Do not scold people for taking too many shells. There's no solid evidence to suggest that removing unoccupied seashells from a beach is going to harm the environment in any way. Only a tiny fraction of the seashells in the ocean makes it to the beach, so there's plenty left in the sea. More importantly, though, trying to shame someone else for getting excited and taking a whole bucket of seashells is just petty. If you feel a strong conviction about "over-shelling," then make the personal choice to stop taking them. You can't control the behavior of others. As well, if you

When I found my first little neon cutie like this one, I used the Shellinators page to obtain a proper identification: rose murex.

aren't a shell collector, no good can come of you being involved with a shell collecting page.
- Stop asking "Was it alive?" The vast majority of beachcombers in the forums know how to distinguish between seashells that are occupied and unoccupied. It's very insulting to ask if they made an unethical choice because that's so far away from anything they would ever consider, and in asking you just might alienate a very knowledgeable sheller who otherwise might have helped you in the future.
- Make sure the tone of all of your posts and comments is positive. Online seashell forums are not the place to complain and vent. Know your audience, because in the case of hobby Facebook groups, people are there to learn.

Finally, while social media makes us feel like we're connected to each other, the truth is that no computer screen is ever going to replace human interaction. We also need to talk to each other in person to learn. That's why you should join a shell club and visit as many seashell shows and fossil festivals as you can. When you get proper identifications from experts on species that stumped you, remember to mark those items with a label including the correct names so you won't forget. And take every opportunity available to you to attend shelling lectures.

Dr. O's Bucket List Species

Because everybody's bucket list is unique and because so many different regions of the country have varied species that are at the top of sheller wish lists, this section focuses only on the most commonly prized species in the United States. If you love augers, apologies are extended in advance because there's no chapter about them here. Maybe they can reflect on their performance, work harder to impress the judges, and make the cut in the second edition of this book. As well, some ultra-rare species that most shellers are unlikely to ever find (like the paper nautilus and the purple janthina) are not featured because the probabilities are not working in anybody's favor on shells like those. Each chapter explains with specifics where you have the best chances of finding these most coveted species. While there are many other sources that will list all of the details about individual shell varieties (like their specific measurements and the habitats of the live creatures), the experts are largely tight-lipped about the actual beaches where your probabilities of finding them will be highest. Also keep in mind that the suggestions offered here are by no means exhaustive. Location guidance is offered in an effort to put you in the best area to find your desired shell. That doesn't mean there's no chance of you finding that prized specimen somewhere else. The sea does as she wishes, and sometimes she likes to keep us guessing. The species that follow are listed in order of their rarity, with the most rare first.

My first purple janthina was found at Anne's Beach in the middle Florida Keys while I was commando crawling underneath a boardwalk looking for sea beans. It was the happiest surprise.

Junonias

The junonia is one of the most coveted and certainly most attractive seashells in America. While there are other seashells that are harder to find, the junonia has gained a reputation as the holy grail for most shellers. Many people live in southwest Florida (where you are most likely to find them) their whole lives and never gain admission to the J club, the name for the fraternity of beachcombers who have discovered even just a piece of this elusive shell.

Fresh junonia shells are peach with very dark brown dots and sometimes a bit of orange on the southbound end. Most of the junonia finds, however, are of whiter sun-bleached specimens with faded dots. The photograph here illustrates the transition from vibrance to sun-bleached fade to beach-worn patina moving left to right.

Even junonia pieces have value, as the shell shops in Florida buy them from locals in order to make jewelry. Live junonias prefer the deep water, which is one of the reasons why they're so random when found on the beach. Sanibel, Florida, has become famous as the single best location for junonias, but posts from all around the southwestern part of the state indicate that people find them with some regularity. Beyond Florida, they occasionally roll up on the Gulf Coast as far over as Alabama, and northward through Georgia and the Carolinas. Cobbs and pieces are found throughout these

I wish I could have met this beauty in his earlier days before life in the ocean took its toll. Even though it sounds strange, most shellers celebrate finding even a piece or a cobb of a junonia. There's no other shell in the country that inspires people to save the incomplete pieces and photograph them.

coastal regions, but often the people don't recognize what they are in beach communities that don't have junonia fever.

Some of you may have come to this book specifically for advice about where to find your first junonia. While the entire Gulf Coast around to the Atlantic and up into the Carolinas might cough up the prize, you want to invest your time and your vacation dollars in a place where junonias are *most likely to emerge*. That place is definitely the west coast of Florida. Social media chatter is one good indicator for you to monitor since beach conditions change all the time. Most people who find their first Js tend to want to post about it, so you can learn all kinds of location information from those announcements. The zone between the Ten Thousand Islands up to Sanibel (to include Marco Island and Keewaydin Island) is really the best hunting ground. Whole junonias also surface in Lido Key (particularly on South Lido) and in Pass-a-Grille. The beach at Cape San Blas is covered in pieces of the shell, and locals report that junonias are there especially after a storm washes up big whole shells.

After hunting locations, the next most common junonia question relates to where on the beach a sheller should be looking. The majority of junonias are found in the water, some by snorkelers and others by shellers walking in the water either using a scooper to investigate interesting shells on the ocean floor or taking advantage of very clear surf to scan the bottom with the naked eye. Just like any other shell, junonias sometimes wash up on the beach. Many beachcombers find them at the high dry wrack line. Oftentimes the customers on chartered shelling tours in Florida will book those excursions for the sole purpose of scoring a junonia, so the captains there are very cognizant of where the most recent shells have been located. Most of these guides are also willing to give you specific junonia hunting advice on the boat ride out to your destination. They often know the honey holes on the particular islands you'll be visiting where junonias seem more likely to wash out, so always ask.

They say that you don't find junonias—they find you. Whatever beach you're hunting, keep your eyes open for the distinctive polka dots. You never know when it's going to be your day to join the club.

Within the larger palette of other shells you'll find in America, there's really nothing else that looks even remotely like the junonia. Because of its larger size and its distinctive color pattern, it's not a shell that goes unnoticed. While shellers might not know exactly what they've found when they pull one out of the surf, the junonia presents itself in a way that lets you know it's something special.

Scotch Bonnets

Scotch bonnets are incredibly desirable but so tricky to find, mainly because there are only a few pockets where they wash out with any regularity. While Scotchies are the state shell of North Carolina, statistically speaking you're really going to find them only in a few locations in the Outer Banks, many of which require a boat to access. If you locate one elsewhere in the Carolinas, you should buy a lottery ticket that day. Two other recommendations for your Scotch bonnet quest are Palm Beach County and Cape San Blas in Florida. Scotch bonnets are structurally delicate, so they break very easily in the surf, and if they're sucked up through the machines that pump sand on the beach for renourishment projects, they get blasted to bits. They tend to roll on an incoming tide, so always check the high wrack line for them.

Most Scotch bonnets are sun-bleached. It's difficult to find them with their colorful dots still present.

Lion's Paws

The lion's paw is a really select shell—one that's in the top five on the bucket list for most shellers. They aren't easy to find, which makes their discovery all the more momentous. You have to know which beaches to search, and because of their size and grandeur, they're scooped up quickly by the first people who come through. They'll overcome you as soon as you see them. Lion's paws are in the scallop family, but they're unusual because they have these round bubbles (or knuckles) on their ridges. You're likely to find more brightly colored orange ones in Florida and darker fossilized ones as you move up toward the Carolinas. If you're in the states between Florida and North Carolina, though, lion's paws are scarce.

There's no such thing as too many lion's paws.

Flat Scallops

Bottom line: flat scallops are the heart's desire of every sheller. Most beachcombers walk right past "flatties" not realizing they're any different from the basic rounded scallops that are available on pretty much every beach. The shells are so flat they can't actually fully close with the animal inside of them. Flats aren't abundant anywhere, but Florida is an excellent place to try your hand. The zone between Palm Beach County on the Atlantic coast all the way over to Navarre on the Gulf coast is prime. Holden Beach, North Carolina, is a notable location for them too.

When I say "flat," I mean really flat. You can barely see the flat scallop in profile.

I was shook when this orange flat scallop called my name from a shell bed early one morning in North Carolina. A flat scallop with such an energetic orange color is a rarity indeed.

Horse Conchs

Among all of the bucket list shells, the horse conch is definitely the largest and for many one of the hardest to find. When you see the shells fully exposed on the beach, they're almost always occupied and need to stay there. When they're buried or rolling around in the water, they're usually empty. If there's an animal inside, they can keep themselves stationary on the ocean floor. Horse conchs are also one of those feast or famine shells. You can go years and never find one, but if you hit a beach just right after a storm, you might discover more than it's possible to carry. They can be found anywhere in the Southeast, but you'll do best with them from Sanibel southward into the Ten Thousand Islands. The big storms and even lower-grade wind events can churn them up, but they're so large that the first beachcombers who get out there are going to take them all. Your footprints just need to be first on the receding tide.

Uninhabited horse conchs are most often buried, so you must train your eyes to look for their "knuckles" sticking out of the sand. Sometimes all you can see is one knob protruding. The southern point of Keewaydin Island is an astounding place for them.

Cones

No beachcomber walks past a cone of any kind and leaves it there. They're a phenomenal seashell. You can find more than thirty varieties of them in the United States, so you'll never get bored with the species. It's smart to pick up every cone shell by the top, avoiding the aperture with your fingers until you know whether or not the shell is occupied. The animals in cone shells can actually sting you. Some of the cones in other parts of the world are venomous. It's said that the sting from the cones in Florida is akin to that of a wasp, but who wants to find out?

The two most common kinds of cones are the alphabet cone (pictured above) and the Florida cone. Shellers go nuts over the "alphies" because of their beauty but also because the brown dot designs on the outside of the shell often form letters or sometimes even whole words. Many beachcombers spend lifetimes trying to find a cone that represents every letter of the English alphabet. Both Florida cones and alphabets are found aplenty in southwest Florida. Keewaydin and Marco Island are ground zero.

Note the prominent "N" in the middle of this chocolate alphabet cone. Can you make out any other letters?

Because the peculiar designs on cones make them stand out on the dry sand or in a shell bed, if even one beachcomber has walked ahead of you, there may be none left. In that case, you need to be looking for them in the water. They roll around there as the tide is moving in and out, and sometimes you'll see just a few polka dots exposed in the sand and need to dig to retrieve the shell.

The golden banded cone is rarer than the junonia. I have never found one in my entire career, and I know only one person who has. My friend Cheryl Carrier discovered the extraordinary specimen pictured above in Florida, but unfortunately her shell collection was swept away in Hurricane Ian. I'm grateful that she shared the photograph and her memories of the shell with me. I hope she finds another one soon to replace it.

Florida cones with the solid orange hue are known as carrot cones, for obvious reasons.

Helmets

There are many American beaches where you might find a helmet, but in most places the chances are very slim. Smaller helmets, which are sometimes called "baby helmets," can be found in the Jupiter, Florida, area. It's a windfall if you find one per walk there. If you're in the market for a bigger helmet, your best opportunity will be either searching in the water in the Outer Banks of North Carolina or snorkeling in the Florida Keys. The prime North Carolina hunting location is on the point at Shackleford Island before you wrap around to the ocean-facing side of the island. All helmets are impressive shells, and any day you find one will be memorable indeed.

Helmets come in a variety of species, including this petite version found on the east coast of Florida. It was the size of a quarter. Loved it. Had to have it.

Tuns

The tun shell is a unicorn, and very many shellers keep their fingers and toes crossed for years waiting for their chance to have one in hand. There's a strange pocket of them (though rare) in the North Carolina Outer Banks and to some extent coming down to the lower beaches of the North Carolina coast into South Carolina. Aside from that, the tun is mostly a tropical shell, so the Florida Keys are a prime target area if you want to find one in the United States.

This sun-bleached tun popped up to say hello in south Florida. I said hello right back.

Floridian snorkeling is a great way to increase your chances. As well, if you can pinpoint one of those places in the Keys where you can walk out a long distance in shallow water with solid sand (and not the sand with the squishy, sinking texture), you might find a tun waiting there. They rarely make it to the beach intact, as they are surprisingly thin and delicate.

The best tun in my collection is this adorable juvenile specimen found in the middle Florida Keys.

Cowries

Cowries look like eggs and are probably the most difficult seashell to distinguish in a shell bed if the aperture side is down. They look exactly like rocks. Unless you're in Florida, they're very unlikely finds, and even in Florida, they aren't exactly bountiful. Snorkelers have the advantage in finding them in calm, clear water. The North Carolina Outer Banks crank them out occasionally. The best beach for finding them on the shore without having to snorkel is Fort Zachary Taylor State Park in Key West, Florida. They range from nickel to softball size. If Mother Nature tosses you a cowrie, treasure it forever.

This old man must have stories to tell, and I would sit and listen to all of them. The openings on cowries look like goofy smiles, which adds to their appeal.

Even with the aperture side up, cowries can still be completely incognito in a shell line. The grooves that look like teeth on the shell opening are an important feature to study while you train your eyes for them.

Caribbean Vases

Finding a Caribbean vase shell will turn any frown into a smile. If you have a week to walk the beaches in the lower Florida Keys, you can usually find two or three of them. The American shell books say they're a southeast Florida/ Keys shell, but they are sometimes located in the Ten Thousand Islands in southwest Florida. Most are minis (about an inch long), but every now and then one in the three-inch range will introduce itself. The extra coloring on the periostracum gives each shell its own character. Your assignment for next class is to book a trip to the Florida Keys to find your own vase shell. Visiting Fort Zachary Taylor State Park will increase your chances of hitting the Caribbean vase lottery.

I have had the great fortune of finding two Caribbean vase shells on the west coast of Florida. It's a bit of an anomaly for them to be that far removed from the Keys.

Sundials

Sundials are extraordinary yet painfully scant. Most expert shellers have only a few in their collections—and that's if they have a chance to hunt the handful of beaches in America with the best chances of them washing ashore. Every now and then you'll see a social media post about a sundial popping up somewhere random, but the Juno Beach Pier in Jupiter, Florida, is probably the place with the most sundial opportunity. Even so, they are remarkably few and far between. Sundials look like cone shells that have been flattened out. You can see how narrow their profile is in the picture below.

Sundials are among the rarest gifts from the sea. Don't let the occasion of finding one pass by without giving thanks or else Mother Nature might not throw you another one.

Wentletraps

Wentletraps are sneaky little shells because they're so small and unassuming, yet they wiggle into the hearts of collectors. If you're a wentletrap devotee, your passion for these spiraling beauties runs deep. They come in varied colors like white, off-white, gray, and brown. There are all kinds of wentletrap varieties that can be found on American beaches, but South Carolina is a prime spot for them. Litchfield Beach is particularly good for some reason. Because of their minute size, you really have to be a micro shell hunter to see them. This requires a vision adjustment away from the larger shells that most beachcombers desire. Because of this, 99 percent of shellers are going to pass right over wentletraps and not realize they're anything significant. But golly, they are special indeed.

After you find that first tiny wentletrap, you won't be able to stop thinking about finding your second one.

Moon Snails

Who doesn't love a good moon snail? Also known as shark's eyes, these beauties can be found on beaches all across America. The prettier ones take up residence in southwest Florida, but bigger ones live in the Carolinas. The especially blue ones are called Paul Newmans. You can find them deposited on the beach and at a low tide rolling around in the water. Most of them are around quarter-sized, but they sometimes grow to be as big as baseballs. If a very small creature decides to adopt one as its home, it can really climb back

Moon snails eat clams and other snails—including other moon snails. Their cannibalism is on full display with the tell-tale bore hole in the shell above.

Fun fact: Moon snails reproduce by laying an egg casing that they perch atop. Sometimes you can find the rubbery egg rings afterward.

in there and hide, so be sure to check them thoroughly before taking them from the beach. For some reason, almost every one found in coastal Georgia is occupied by a tiny critter. On the flip side, it's unusual to find an occupied one north of there.

Olives

Olives are a variety of shell that's really prized among collectors who live in areas where they aren't normally found. If you have easy access to the Grand Strand of South Carolina, you know that olives are incredibly commonplace, so they might not push your buttons necessarily. The most prevalent variety is the lettered olive, but their colors vary wildly due to beach exposure and fossilization and might include black, blue, orange, red, and even hints of purple and green. Siesta Key on the Gulf side of Florida produces the darkest olives anywhere, while the eastern side of the state will toss you the more warm-colored ones. The best part of the olive shell in good condition is its ultra-glossy finish. You don't need to do anything to clean an olive shell except rinse it with water.

Sand trails like this mean that a live olive is on a mission to get somewhere. This chap was taking care of business on Marco Island, Florida.

There are a few variations of the olive shell that collectors scramble to find. The top of that list is the rare golden olive (pictured on the left). Golden olives have no pattern and are a very distinctive warm yellow color. They're different from sun-bleached lettered olives, which often still bear faint markings that you can see if you look closely enough.

Angelwings

Angelwings are so paper thin that it's a wonder how they get washed onto the beach without breaking. If you're fortunate enough to find a perfect one, you'll need to have a plan for the commute home that doesn't involve the angelwing rolling around in your shell bucket with the rest of your finds. Angelwings can pop up anywhere, but the greatest concentration noted in the shelling forums is at Onslow Beach, North Carolina. Southwest Florida also usually delivers with them. The one in the picture below is quite large—six inches or so. Crafters go bananas for them because they're handy in art projects. As you can imagine, they make for pretty shell angels around the holidays.

The angelwing is an exceedingly delicate shell. Finding one intact is a triumph.

There are a few different varieties of angelwings found in the Southeast, including the "false" angelwing (pictured on the right). That distinction is difficult to discern and really doesn't matter to me. They're all just pretty.

Angelwings look very much like a common ark shell, so they blend in with basic shell hash. You want to train your eye to look for the ridges but in a much longer form because the angelwing is a very wide shell.

Whelks

Whelks rank so high up on most sheller wish lists because of their size. Outside of a jumbo horse conch, whelks are really the biggest shells you'll find washed up on the beach. One of the main impetuses for moving as quickly as possible in the morning before the sun comes up is to snag the big whelks that have washed ashore in the night. Even as you hunt, be sure to keep a lookout very far ahead of you down the beach and look backward occasionally because the sizable ones appear out of nowhere with strong waves.

One unusual thing about whelks is that there isn't really a centralized place where the best ones are located. Superb examples can be found all over the United States.

Big whelks are available on nearly every beach in America. I'm addicted to them. These fellows are GONE as soon as the sun comes up because they're so conspicuous.

So many beachcombers flock to the coast for a showcase seashell, and usually it's a whelk they picture in their minds. Therefore, whelks are an ideal shell to give away to kiddos who are on the hunt. Or if you still have thirty of them in your trunk from the last time you hunted and you haven't even cleaned them, maybe you could use the ones you see on the beach to teach visitors how to find them.

There are many varieties of whelks, but we'll go through a few identifications by using pictures to learn. The knobbed whelk (pictured above) has fancy pointed knobs that make the shell highly collectible if found intact. Unfortunately, wave action usually breaks off those knobs and rubs them down.

The lightning whelk (pictured above on the left) has an aperture opening on the left instead of the right. Remember "left for lightning."

Pear whelks have very pleasing wavy stripes and short spires.

Channel whelks come with stupendous polka dots on the edges, and the spire builds up like a castle. The best ones have a purple tint and yellow/brown dots like the ones above.

Tulips

Shellers with any amount of experience have probably reached the point where they have to acknowledge they have a problem: there are only so many banded tulips a reasonable person should possess. If buckets of them are lining the walls of your garage, it's probably time for an intervention. The thing that makes them so hard to resist is that each one is a little bit different with its pattern and coloring, which really adds to the feeling that you need them all in your life. The banded tulip is most common. They're found occasionally in North and South Carolina, fairly often in Georgia, commonly in Florida, and every now and then in Mississippi and Alabama. They're abundant from Sanibel, Florida, southward to the Everglades. If it's time for you to admit you have a banded tulip collecting problem, one solution is to hand them

Ah, the chocolate true tulip. It's better than dessert.

Pretty, pretty, pretty. True tulips are the bee's knees.

This live true tulip stopped me in my tracks on Keewaydin Island, Florida. Once I realized he was alive, I quickly snapped a picture and put him right back in the water.

out to neighborhood kids at Halloween in addition to candy. Don't short the trick-or-treaters on the candy.

The less common kind of tulip shell is the true tulip. Its colors range from red to orange to chocolatey brown. Sometimes shellers get confused about whether they have a banded tulip or a true tulip. The trick to telling the difference is to rub the side of the shell. If the surface is smooth, it's a banded tulip. If the surface is textured, it's a true tulip.

Nutmegs

So here's the rule. When you find a nutmeg, you have to holler, "Nutty nutmeg!" Nutmeg shells are little balls of the best kind of fun. They have similar shape and coloring as Scotch bonnets, so they're commonly confused but actually not related to each other. On the whole, nutmegs are much smaller than Scotchies. Some beaches are better for them than others (like Cape San Blas, Florida). Because of their small size, you really need a trained eye to spot them. It's the raised-dot texture that will help you teach your eyes to discern them.

When the answer to your husband asking "What in the world is wrong with the washing machine?" turns out to be a handful of nutmegs, and you're the only person in the house with a weakness for nutmegs, you can't hide your guilt.

Murexes

The two most common kinds of murexes are the apple and the lace. You'll find them occasionally throughout the Southeast, but Florida is where their population really explodes. When you get into the Ten Thousand Islands, particularly on Kice Island for some reason, you'll discover that murexes are as available as ark shells and cockles on most other beaches.

The apple murexes pictured here have alternating segments of brown and white color. Apple murexes are small shells—no more than two or three inches. Just because they're easy to find doesn't mean that they lack pizzazz, though.

The lighter colored lace murexes are extremely difficult to see in Florida's white-tinted shell hash. Their sharp spines make the edges look like lace. They're dainty and fabulous. The prettiest ones have a peach-colored top.

The murex congeniality award belongs to the Cabrit's murex (pictured above). The Marco / Keewaydin Island area of Florida will offer you more murexes than any other stretch of beach.

One of the reasons I'm so drawn to beach collecting is that my overactive imagination prompts me to marvel at the story each seashell tells. I want to know who lived in this rose murex and what kind of happiness amplified his neon-orange color.

Where things get really interesting with the murex is in the more rare species. The hardest to find is the Cabrit's murex, which is pictured on the previous page (bottom left). The beach-worn specimens are going to have broken-off spines, but when the animal is alive, the shell has fairly long spikes down its pointy-looking tail.

The spikes of the lavish giant murex are enough to make you swoon. When they do announce themselves, my goodness, they make quite an entrance. If you find one that isn't sun-bleached, the stripes on it will wear you out. However, any murex that's added to your collection is a blessing.

This is why my house is always going to have at least a little bit of sand on the floor. I never can seem to get it all out before bringing the shells in from the beach. This giant murex is about six inches long. Everybody who visits my house has to spend time with it. If you come over, I'll show it to you.

Tellins

It's obvious why shell collectors go bananas over tellins. In the case of the rose tellin (pictured to the right), aside from the inside lip of a mature queen conch, there aren't very many other things on the beach that pack such an intense pink punch. Beyond their apparent beauty, rose tellins are also very high on most sheller bucket lists because they're concentrated in a minute area of Florida. The tip of north Marco Island is your target zone for them. As a result, the rose tellin has gained the reputation as Marco Island's signature shell. Park at Tigertail Beach and start hiking toward the north point. Be sure to also check the highest storm surge wrack lines up in the very dry sand. Tellins come in a variety of species and colors, and all of them are easiest to find in Florida.

Can you spot the rose tellin in the knockout rose? The full common name of the shell is the "rose petal tellin" for good reason.

Not to be outdone, the sunrise tellin variety (pictured in the center above) is a bit of a show-off, too. These lookers were found in Bahia Honda, Florida.

Spiny and Leafy Jewelboxes

Jewelboxes are super fancy bivalves (animals with two shells hinged together). They're almost always found detached, but sometimes you'll score two shells still fused together. The spiny jewelbox has elegant spines that are rarely found fully intact. If you're hunting a beach with rough surf, the spiny jewelboxes will have dotted nubs instead of spines. The spiniest jewelboxes around seem to like the

These two hunks took my breath away one morning on Lido Key. There's romance in this kind of beauty.

Sarasota, Florida, area. Take a plastic container with you on the beach to make sure none of them break before you can get them back to the house. The leafy jewelboxes are gloriously colorful. Instead of spikes, they have leafy-looking scales (hence the name). Leafy jewelboxes with intact leaves abound in the Florida Keys. You can find beach-worn jewelboxes in many locales, but the perfect specimens are infrequent.

This purple leafy jewelbox was found in Key West, Florida. You can pick up jewelboxes elsewhere in the Southeast, but the Sunshine State seems to have the best colors and quality.

You can't miss this bold canary yellow when you're scanning the ocean floor for dainties. I was ecstatic to find this leafy jewelbox with both sides attached. Be aware that even if you get attached bivalves home safely, once they dry out, the hinge won't flex anymore without breaking. Get them immediately into a display case, and don't touch them.

Crown Conchs

Crown conchs (sometimes called king crowns) are ornate treasures. The white stripes across the shell are dazzling, and their spikes give the shell the appearance of a crown, which inspired its moniker. The corridor between Sanibel and the Ten Thousand Islands in Florida is their stomping ground. Crown conchs also like to congregate on the bay sides of islands, so you can find them away from "the beach" as well. They seem to assemble in large numbers around Sanibel, so if this is a species you need to knock off the list, that's where you should focus.

Most crown conchs are tumbled and worn. The bucket list shellers are on the hunt for the ones with spines intact and a darker color instead of the faded caramel.

Other Notable Beach Finds

Shark Teeth

If you're serious about learning how to find shark teeth on the beach, you need to pick up my 2015 book *Shark Tooth Hunting on the Carolina Coast*. It will teach you where to hunt, how to hunt, and how to identify the species with an all-color identification guide. What's offered here, though, is a quick summary of the most important tips to get you started.

First, 95 percent of the shark teeth you will find on a beach are black because that is the most common color for fossilized teeth in the United States. Brown, gray, and cream-colored teeth pop out on the beach too, but they represent a very small percentage of the total available. You want to play the percentages when you first start hunting, so begin by training your eyes on every black thing you see in the shell hash. You're going to pick up a lot of things that turn out to not be shark teeth, including pieces of oyster shell and unidentifiable bone fragments. Don't be discouraged, and keep trying.

Second, you want to focus on objects in the shell hash that are pointed and triangular. A shark tooth will have a dull root at the top and shiny enamel on the "tooth" (as illustrated in the picture above).

You also want to make sure you're hunting on a beach where shark teeth are known to wash out because not every beach has them. This book has talked so much about the tremendous shelling in Sanibel and Marco Island, Florida, but you're not going to find a shark tooth there because there's no fossil record with shark teeth washing out. North Carolina beaches like

Topsail, Onslow, Holden, and Ocean Isle and South Carolina beaches like Cherry Grove and Edisto are recommended if you're exclusively interested in finding shark teeth.

It's also beneficial to start your shark tooth journey on the beach with an experienced hunter. That person can find a few teeth, show them to you before picking them up, and put them down ahead of you later so you can begin to teach your eyes what to see.

Once you get in the habit of looking for black and pointed things on the sandy surface, teeth like these will jump up and smack you in the face. When I saw this great white shark tooth minding its own business in the shell hash, I sucked in so much air that I almost choked on my own spit.

She's a little broken up, but aren't we all in one way or another? Megalodon shark teeth that you find on the beach have either washed out of their original formation and tumbled around in the surf or been sucked up through machines and spread around with earth-moving equipment after a beach renourishment project. Therefore, the bigger teeth will usually be damaged like the one in the picture. Most of the pristine teeth that wind up for sale in beach shops and online were retrieved by underwater divers.

Sea Beans

If you've never hunted sea beans before, you have to start today, and get your kids and grandkids involved because it's one of the most intriguing beach hobbies. Sea beans are highly durable seed pods that fall off vines, shrubs, and trees and then float (sometimes for decades and thousands of miles) before they land on another beach. The best place to find them in America is in the Florida Keys or on the west side or the Panhandle of Florida. An argument could be made for the Texas Gulf coast being a very close second runner-up. Look in the high wrack line in the plant debris because they tend to get popped in the air with the waves, and then they roll. Days that are extra seaweedy are the best time to be on patrol. Amazingly, these sea pods will still sprout—even if they've been adrift for a hundred years or more. The

And this is how it all starts. You spot that first sea heart, and you're a goner. The best place to search for sea beans is at the high wrack line or the last place the highest tide was. It's easier to distinguish sea beans in dried seaweed instead of in the bigger piles of green seaweed that just washed ashore. After the seaweed spends a few days on the beach it wilts, making the beans very evident.

Without question, the best place to find sea beans is the Florida Keys. You want to hunt the Atlantic side instead of the Gulf side for morsels like this hamburger bean.

sprout will likely not thrive and mature if you take it home to a nontropical climate, but it's still fun to try. Many of these pods come from Central and South America, and based on the appearance of the bean, you can use the free online sea bean charts to figure out where they originated. This is the part that children need to be involved in: hunt with them and then help them research so they can collect beans from all over the world. Some of the rare sea beans can be very difficult to find, so this can really turn into an exciting lifetime pursuit. Find a comprehensive sea bean chart online and start studying. Our quiz will be next week.

There is no argument: All sea bean hunters want a Mary's bean. I have only found two in my career. This brown variety is super rare.

Indigenous Artifacts

You have to be ready for anything when you're beachcombing, and when it's your day to find an artifact left behind by an Indigenous person from long ago, you want to make sure your eyeballs are ready to see it before someone else does. Most beach hunters find their first arrowheads quite by accident because they have their eyes conditioned to look for shark teeth. Shark teeth and points (a slang term for arrowheads) often have both shape and color in common. Arrowheads are such significant finds that few collectors ever sell them, and if you happen to score one and post

This picture demonstrates why so many shark tooth hunters find arrowheads and the shellers often miss them. The item in the center is an arrowhead, and it is flanked by two shark teeth.

it on social media, be prepared for the sales offers to pour into your message box. If you haven't spent any time learning about local artifacts, you should find a collecting group keyed to your state on Facebook. There are a lot of Indigenous artifacts found on beaches, and many of them look just like rocks if you aren't familiar with the distinguishing features. By seeing pictures and identifications from finds in your state, you'll begin to learn about the characteristics that should catch your eye on the beach. Also be aware that state parks in some coastal areas prohibit the removal of artifacts related to Indigenous people, so acquaint yourself with the rules wherever you hunt. When you do find one of these remnants of the past, stop and appreciate its significance. An artisan thousands of years ago crafted an object that's so graceful in its design yet so useful and vital to existence. It survived all that time in the exact same condition and landed in your hand. It doesn't get much better than that, friends.

Military Artifacts

It's always helpful to know the history of the beaches you hunt because that information can help you prepare for the location-specific goodies you have the capacity to find there. One of those rarities is spent bullet casings from military training. Holden Beach, North Carolina, where the U.S. military trained for World War II, is an excellent place to hunt for them. You can pick up fifty-caliber shells there like the big ones in the photo above. The bullets that wash out at Holden are mostly from the 1940s. Most of them either were blanks to begin with or were live rounds that were fired and thus are not dangerous. The blanks are distinguished by a little crinkle in the metal

This bullet casing found at Onslow Beach has a year stamp (60) on the bottom, meaning it was manufactured in 1960. The "L C" stands for Lake City Ordnance Plant in Independence, Missouri.

at the top. Bullet casings are also abundant on Onslow Beach, which is on the Camp Lejeune Marine Corps base. The majority of the casings there are from the 1960s to the 1990s. Military bullets are extremely collectible because they're stamped on the bottom with the date and the initials of the factory where they were manufactured. You can find free charts online that will tell you what city the initials correspond to, which is a really fun research project for youngsters who are interested in military history. Finding them is like discovering a little time capsule. As with shark teeth, once you spot that first bullet casing, you'll see them everywhere if you're on a beach where they wash out. The best part is that these artifacts are surface finds—items found on the beach without digging, sifting, or metal detecting. The bullet casings tend to wash out after storms in pockets, probably because a soldier with a large gun was in the same spot spraying many bullets all at one time. It's so exciting to see a wave retreat with ten or twelve bullets scattered around you.

Sea Glass

Sea glass hunting is another one of those splinter beachcombing groups with its own diehard community. Sea glass is a piece of broken glass that has become weathered and frosty from its time rolling around in the ocean.

Its colors vary widely, and collectors are always on the hunt for specific rare colors like black, yellow, orange, and red. Many crafters are desperate for as much sea glass as they can get their hands on for jewelry making. If you are purchasing sea glass in bulk or in jewelry, be sure to ask if it is naturally weathered or machine-tumbled, as most people prefer pieces that have been created by the sea instead of a rock tumbling device.

Sometimes you'll find a shard of a brown beer bottle that could have been broken by a beach reveler the night before. That's not sea glass. True sea glass will be worn with smoothed edges and a cloudy appearance.

Many of the same strategies that are used to read the beach in seashell and fossil hunting hold true for sea glass hunting. Learning to train your eye for the distinct shapes and textures of sea glass is your first tool. You'll begin to recognize the colors of glass that are most frequently found in the locations you visit, and your eyes will become drawn to those hues over time. For instance, the Bahamas and the Florida Keys are known for their abundance of aqua blue sea glass. Receding tides are an optimal time to grab sea glass, particularly on beaches with strong wave action or in places that have recently experienced a storm. Location is also paramount, as some shores are loaded

This pair of photographs demonstrates the difference between actual sea glass that has a worn, frosty appearance and smooth edges (left) and pieces of freshly broken glass found on a beach (right). The line between trash and treasure is a thin one indeed in the world of sea glass.

with sea glass while others have none. One of the best sea glass hunting locations in the country is the southern-facing side of Key West, Florida. Just be sure to wear shoes to protect yourself from hazards in the water. There are outstanding places to search for sea glass all over the coastal United States, so always give it a try if you are anywhere near the water.

Often the highest concentration of sea glass you'll find is on a rocky beach. It also helps if those rocks are white, like the coral rocks found on Caribbean shores. You can spot the bright pops of the sea glass colors in contrast to the light background. Even on days when there isn't much shelling action, you can almost always collect a nice handful of sea glass, especially if you find a spot where nobody else has thought to look. Your visual strategy will need to shift if you're combing a beach with darker-colored rocks, shell hash, pebbles, or just blank sand because that backdrop will make it harder to distinguish the colors you want.

As you're out scouring the beaches for glass each day, pick up and dispose of any sharp broken glass you see (especially the clear variety that will go undetected by most people). Nobody wants to get foot stitches, so one of the nicest things you can do for other families on vacation is remove that potential danger from the beach. While your eyes are trained on manmade objects, also be on the lookout for marbles, pieces of dishware, and Indigenous pottery shards. If you have even an ounce of inquisitiveness, you will likely latch on to sea glass hunting in short order. Each new piece will set your imagination on fire as you try to figure out what it was originally and how old it might be.

The more desirable pieces of sea glass include bottle lips and pieces with some sort of texture or visible lettering. Your hunting will move to the next level if you can scout out locations that used to be landfills or dumps or beaches that are adjacent to such sites. That is where quirky things like collectible old bottles might be rolling around in the surf.

Sea Biscuits

Sea biscuit is the common name for a kind of echinoid. Other echinoids include sea urchins and sand dollars. There are several kinds of sea biscuits found in America. The one pictured to the right is from a beach renourishment in Holden Beach in 2022 that produced thousands of these Cretaceous wonders. Ocean Isle, North Carolina, also delivers them with some regularity. The larger Caribbean species of sea biscuits can be found while snorkeling in the Florida Keys. Outside of a beach renourishment project that stirs up a large quantity of sea biscuits, they're otherwise a pretty random find. You might stumble upon a whole one every two or three years. A

These sea biscuits were found in the Florida Keys. Very often they'll be damaged like the one on the right, but you can also find them whole.

good dredging project on a stretch of coastline can spoil us for a few years when sea biscuit availability seems endless, but we shouldn't lose sight of how special they are.

Me: "I will not pick up any more sea biscuits. I will not pick up any more sea biscuits. I will not pick up any more sea biscuits. I will not pick up any more sea biscuits. I will not pick up any more sea biscuits."

Also me: "Look how pretty this one is" (while picking up another sea biscuit).

Sand Dollars

When most people think of the ocean, one of the first images that comes to mind is a sand dollar. However, they elude a lot of shellers who don't recognize the best places to find them or what to look for when they're mostly hidden in the sand. Sometimes people on a quest for their first sand dollar say, "I've looked my entire life and have never found one. How do you find so many?" The answer is usually that the person asking is hunting exclusively on vacation on the same beach—a beach that isn't known to have sand dollars. The location chapter earlier in this book provided some great leads that should put you on top of as many sand dollars as you could possibly want. You can't go wrong with Jekyll Island, Georgia, and Tigertail Beach, Florida. Anywhere from Pass-a-Grille southward on the west coast of Florida will also satisfy your sand dollar itch.

These dead sand dollars were collected in coastal Alabama. Notice some of the edges are broken. Because sand dollars are inordinately fragile, you'll need a plan for getting them back from the beach without breakage. One way to strengthen them is to mix white school glue with an equal amount of water and brush it on both sides of the sand dollar. Let each side dry before you flip it.

Sea Urchins

Sea urchins are one of the most enchanting animals you'll ever encounter on a beach, but they're tricky little suckers. Unless you want to invest your time in a lot of foul-smelling work, make sure you bring home only the tests (or the hard shells without the animals in them). The spines will have fallen off, and the shell will be very lightweight and ultra-delicate. If it still has spines and you can see an animal inside, there's a chance it's still alive, and they move so slowly that it's nearly impossible to determine if it's truly dead. Some of them will sting you, so you don't want to step on the spines or have them run up under your fingernail. You could potentially find an urchin on any beach you

Once all of the spines are cleaned off the sea urchin, all that remains is the delicate test.

search, but the Carolinas and Florida seem to be hotspots for them. There are days when you'll find more on a beach than you can carry. Urchins don't belong in a bucket with your shells, though. They're much too tender to survive any pressure or weight.

If you do find a dead sea urchin that you'd like to clean, get it home fast in an airtight container because they'll ooze a special kind of stink all up in your car. Soaking them in water for a few hours usually makes the spines come off, and the expired animal will eventually come out of the bottom too.

Depending on the morning, you may find sea urchins washed up all over the beach. You'll often see the birds flipping them over and eating the animal out of the bottom of the shell.

Starfish

Starfish are really old creatures when considered on the timeline of animal life since Earth was created. The public's fascination with them will never wane, and unfortunately the commercial purveyors of sea creatures capitalize on that by keeping beach stores fully stocked with them. The perpetual beachcombers who put in the hours know how rare it is to find a deceased starfish on the beach. That's why when we see a tacky door wreath covered in painted starfish in a gift shop, all we can envision is a ring of death. Those starfish were killed for what turned out to be a pretty hideous decoration. If a starfish is mushy and you know for sure it's dead, feel free to take it.

As my experiences beside the ocean have grown, I've come to realize that not everything wonderful I find has to come home in my shell bucket in order for me to remember the special moments. While I would never scold anyone for "over-shelling," I do like to at least float the idea of admiring and then leaving even dead animals like starfish. Lots of other creatures, including birds, turtles, and crabs, will eat dead starfish.

But please consider the fact that you'll find an equal amount of joy from admiring them beside the ocean and then leaving them be. No touching is the best approach. The starfish pictured on the previous page (top) was actually beached by waves and flipped over. The photo was taken as it was being returned to the water as quickly as possible. If you're in the act of rescue, you can also scoop sand underneath the animal so your skin doesn't actually come in contact with it. That approach would have been better than the way the starfish was handled in the picture. Even the author of this book still learns more humane ways to beachcomb all the time.

Crab Shells and Legs

Beachcombing is about finding something that speaks to your spirit and bringing it home to love forever, even if that something is weird and sometimes makes your car stink. If crab parts are your jam, your family is probably not going to understand, and that's okay. This world is hard, and we have to have those peculiar little obsessions that bring us joy. Happiness for you might come in knowing you have a whole lot of pretty crab shells tucked away in a drawer that you'll never do anything with. There are closeted crab shell groupies all over the globe, so you aren't alone.

Most often crab shells and legs are found at the high wrack line of the beach. They land there after the highest waves of the day deposit them.

The crown jewel for all crab shell collections is the flame box crab. Live flame box crabs like to chill out on sandbars, and boy are they moody. Stunningly beautiful, but moody.

Finding empty horseshoe crab shells on the beach is such a charge (especially if the tail is still attached). If you're planning to take one, though, be prepared for an unspeakable aroma if there's any flesh at all left on the underside of the shell. I came home from a beach trip once, and because of the stench emanating from my closed trunk, my husband was fully convinced there was a decomposing human body in there. Live horseshoe crabs look so foreboding and mean, but they won't hurt you. If you see a live one flipped upside down on the beach, it's safe to help it back to the ocean.

Serendipitous Treasures

Perhaps the best part of beachcombing is the unknown. Despite best efforts, nobody can ever truly predict what will wash up. Mother Nature will always play her cards close to the vest and keep us wondering with each new tide, and that's the part of this hobby that will feed your brain waves forever. Her random surprises come when we least expect them, and our curiosity about the sea is stoked all over again. The veteran beachcombers will tell you they have found a lot of strange things: dentures, cash, car keys, and cell phones. There was also a bizarre morning in Myrtle Beach a few years ago when twenty-six oranges inexplicably washed up on the beach within a half-mile span. But all

of these items are the result of human activity. This quick chapter documents in photos some of the unexpected treasures that actually come from the sea, like the striking egg casing pictured on the previous page. These miraculous moments of discovery often lead the fortunate finders to jump on the research trail for an identification. Seeing pictures of the wonderful and quirky things you might come across on your next beach walk is really important because many of these items are ones that an uninformed beachcomber would walk by without recognizing their value. Your skill development will hopefully bring you to the place where your eyes can simultaneously search for shells, shark teeth, and any other beach trophy that inspires you instead of having to focus on one task as newcomers often do. The serendipitous discoveries documented in this chapter would be great additions to the list of things you want your eyeballs to have the capacity to see.

A mermaid's purse is an egg sac for rays and sharks that do not give live birth. If you see an opening on one of the ends, the sac is vacant, and you can take it. If the purse is enclosed, put it back in the water because the egg might still be viable.

Here's an interesting bit of trivia in case you ever wind up on Jeopardy! and the final category is sea creatures. The hard foot of a shelled creature is called an operculum. The animal uses the operculum to scoot itself through the sand. This one is from a horse conch, and it's extra special because the frilly growth that's hitching a ride on it is actually the egg casing of a banded tulip shell.

The white bony structure on top of this Bahamian sea star is called a crucifix fish (because it looks like a cross). It's actually the skull of a big old catfish called the sailcat. They occasionally wash up on shore, and beachcombers who are drawn to oddities pick them up.

If you ever have the good fortune of collecting a shell with this kind of intricate coral growth on it, please do me a favor and NEVER *clean it. This is a level of perfection that only Mother Nature can achieve, and any human interference in its natural beauty would be criminal.*

If you spend any time on the beach, you'll come across your share of bird feathers, like this divine roseate spoonbill feather. However, the Migratory Bird Treaty Act, which mandates which bird parts you can legally possess, is just about the most convoluted piece of legislation ever written. You'll actually be less confident in what you know about birds after you read it. It's nearly impossible to figure out if one of the exceptions applies to your case, so it's easier to admire the feathers on the beach and leave them behind.

The splendor of the unicorn yellow scallop is unparalleled. If you're a newcomer to the shelling world, it's impossible to know what all of the rarities are. By diving into the online shelling forums and paying attention to the finds that leave people breathless, you'll start to get a feel for the species and varieties that are the most coveted.

I was startled to find this enormous California wavy turban shell tucked in between the rocks at Terramar Beach in Carlsbad, California. I was so lost in the beauty of the rocks that I really wasn't even looking for seashells when this turban presented itself. It's the size of a softball and truly one of the most unexpected joys I've ever experienced on a beach.

Conclusion

It's hard to imagine that after writing this whole book I still have something to say. But I do, and it might be the most salient thing of all. Our culture has fooled us into believing we should always be overcommitted and busy, busy, busy. We're encouraged to wear our burnout as a badge of honor. Multitasking is prized over focus. As the world around us accelerates, humans are losing their ability to hear their own inner voices. The result is a population that's increasingly not equipped to unplug and truly relax their bodies and minds. I think that's where the ocean comes in. I would encourage you to drop something that is weighing you down and use the extra time to go to the beach instead. The beachcomber is a naturally curious soul, and curiosity as a trait is a self-sustaining coping tool. I'm fully convinced that the sea will heal you if you allow it. But to get to that point, you have to let yourself get lost in the wonder of what Mother Ocean deposits on the shore every morning. She'll be your best friend if you let her, and she'll give you the freedom to be yourself in whatever bizarre capacity your true colors might shine. Her gifts are also free for the taking, yet so few of us recognize that generosity. It's a wonderland out there, but your eyes have to be fully open to see it. In doing nothing for a little while, you'll actually be doing the most important thing you could ever do for yourself. Listen to your intuition when it says you need to stop and put some salt air in your lungs. It's that intuition that keeps us alive. Never doubt it.

Your job now is to take what I've offered and go make your own fun. If you don't yet recognize which stretch of coastline brings you the most joy, it would delight me to know that my book helped you find it. I hope that you'll follow my adventures on Facebook by joining the pages "Ultimate Shell Seeker's Guide" and "On the Beach with Dr. Ashley Oliphant." That's where I post content about where I'm hunting, what I'm finding, and what I'm learning. You can also view announcements about my upcoming lectures and classes there. Maybe I'll be coming to your town soon. Now it's time for me to put the "out of office" notice on my email and take my own advice. There's a salty little island calling my name, and those seashells won't find themselves. Happy hunting, friends.

Special Thanks

. . . are due to Beth Yarbrough, my extraordinary mother, who spent more than a hundred hours editing photos for this project. Evidence of your profound talent and creative vision is found in every single picture contained in this volume. They say that what separates the great artists from the rest of the populace is their ability to see the world in a different way. I'll always be amazed at how you can take a great photo into the stratosphere with just a few clicks and adjustments. Life would have been so boring with anybody else as my Mama.

Dr. Cameron Bearder, my superstar chiropractor at Keystone Upper Cervical Spine Clinic in Cornelius, North Carolina, for keeping my head straight on my shoulders as I powered through the final hectic months with this book. You made me believe I was going to be okay, and so I was. Your brilliance continually astonishes me, and I hope you never get so famous that you don't have time to do my neck.

Neighbors Jennifer Baker and Joyce Harper, for allowing me to wander through your yards at all hours because you have better foliage for seashell picture taking.

Fellow shellers Joseph Fusco, Rene Vance, and Cheryl Carrier, for agreeing to share some of your most rare seashells with the rest of the world in this book.

Fossil hunter Justin Kiser, for letting me tag along in your dive boat and learn how it's done. Very few people have what it takes to swim with those Lowcountry gators, and I'm definitely not a member of that elite class.

And John Ryhal, for making me laugh when I need it most and for carrying my shell bucket when it gets heavy.

Works Cited

Bailey-Matthews National Shell Museum. "Shells & Science." March 23, 2024. https://www.shellmuseum.org/shells-science.

Florida Fish and Wildlife Conservation Commission. "Red Tide Current Status." March 23, 2024. https://myfwc.com/research/redtide/statewide/.

Gale, Bob, Pam Gale, and Ashby Gale. *A Beachcomber's Guide to Fossils*. University of Georgia Press, 2020.

Hemingway, Ernest. *By-Line: Ernest Hemingway: Selected Articles and Dispatches of Four Decades*. Edited by William White. Charles Scribner's Sons, 1967.

———. *The Old Man and the Sea*. Charles Scribner's Sons, 1952.

Oliphant, Ashley. *Shark Tooth Hunting on the Carolina Coast*. Pineapple Press, 2015.

Talladega Nights: The Ballad of Ricky Bobby. Directed by Adam McKay, Sony Pictures, 2006.

Witherington, Blair, and Dawn Witherington. *Florida's Living Beaches*. 2nd ed. Pineapple Press, 2017.

———. *Florida's Seashells: A Beachcomber's Guide*. 2nd ed. Pineapple Press, 2017.

———. *Living Beaches of Georgia and the Carolinas: A Beachcomber's Guide*. Pineapple Press, 2011.

Index

AccuWeather, 34
Airbnb, 55
albino shells, 197
Alligator Point, Fla., 102–3
alphabet cone, 91, 99, 222
Amelia Island, Fla., 75
angelwing, 234–35; false, 235
Anne's Beach, Fla., 79, 212
A1A, 78, 145, 199
Apalachicola, Fla., 102–3
aperture, 114, 173, 187–88
apple murex, 242
arc shell, 69
arrowheads, 256–57
Ashley River, 63
auger, 60, 212

Bahia Honda, Fla., 79; state park, 145, 202
Bailey-Matthews National Shell Museum, 205
banded tulip. *See under* tulip
beach hopping, 142–43
beachcombing gear, 177–82
bear spray, 166
berm wall, 136–37
Big Bend, 100, 102, 165
biting fly, 193
biting midge, 192–94
bivalves, 246
bleach soaking, 187–88
Blind Pass Beach (Sanibel, Fla.), 94, 96, 118
Bon Secour Bay, 106
Bonita Beach, Fla., 92
Boulineau's, 58
Bowman's Beach, Fla., 94, 118
BoxBox displays, 189
bugs, 92, 192–94; biting fly, 193; biting midge, 192–94; chiggers, 192–93; mosquitos, 193; No-See-Ums, 192–94
bullet casings, 50
Buxton, N.C., 47

Cabrit's murex, 243–44
California wavy turban, 277
Camp Lejeune Marine Corps Base, 50, 259
Cape Lookout, N.C., 47
Cape Romano, Fla., 86
Cape San Blas, Fla., 101–2, 104, 168, 214, 216
Captiva Island, Fla., 94, 96
Caribbean vase, 38, 228
Carlsbad, Calif., 277
Carrabelle, Fla., 103
carrot cone, 223
channel whelk, 237
Charleston, S.C., 62–65
Cherry Grove, S.C., 58–61, 112, 252; pier, 58, 61, 140
chiggers, 192–93
cilia, 174
clams, 116; coquina, 2
Clearwater, Fla., 100
cobb, 149, 213–14

Cocoa Beach, Fla., 74
cockle, 64
coffee bean trivia, 77
cones, 222–23; alphabet, 91, 99, 222; carrot, 223; Florida cone, 222–23; golden banded, 223; Sozon's, 104
Cooper River, 63
coquina clam, 2
coral, 276
Corsair Beach Park, 70
cowrie, 14, 227
crab, 271–72; flame box, 272; horseshoe, 103, 272
crown conch, 248; king's crown, 156, 248
crucifix fish, 275
Cumberland Island, Ga., 71–73; ferry, 71–73

Dauphin Island, Ala., 106–8, 140
Daytona Beach, Fla., 74, 111
Destin, Fla., 104
Dickman's Island, Fla., 86
digging, 125–27
dolphins, 2, 161
dredging, 42. *See also* renourishment
Dremel tool, 186
Driftwood Beach, Ga., 73

East Coast Fossil Club (Facebook), 206–7
echinoids, 54, 263
Edisto Island, S.C., 64–67, 252; state park, 64
essential oils, 193
ethical beachcombing, 172–76
Everglades, 84–85
excursions, 160–64

false angelwing, 235
Fernandina Beach, Fla., 74
ferries, 23, 47–48, 162–63
fig, 95
fish mouth plate, 41
FITKICKS, 179
flamingo tongue, 153
fog, 168
fossil context, 13
foul weather gear, 32, 35
flashlights, 146–48, 175, 177–78
Florida cone, 222–23
Florida fighting conch, 101
Florida Fish and Wildlife Conservation Commission, 190
Florida Keys, 14, 21, 78–83, 199, 200–201
Folly Beach, S.C., 63
Fort Myers, Fla., 92
Fort Zachary Taylor State Park, 80–81, 83, 202, 227–28
Frisco Beach, N.C., 47

Gale, Bob, Pam, and Ashby, 204
Georgetown, S.C., 58
giant murex, 54, 244
golden banded cone, 223
Golden Isles, Ga., 70–73
golden olive, 233
Goodland, Fla., 86
Grand Strand, 58–61, 115, 233
Green Mill Run, N.C., 159
grounding, 179
Gulf Breeze Motel (Ala.), 108
Gulf Shores, Ala., 104, 106

hamburger bean, 254
Hatteras Island, N.C., 47
headlamps, 146, 166, 175, 177–78
helmet, 49, 224
Hemingway, Ernest, 11
Hemingway Water Shuttle, 90, 149–50, 164
Holden Beach, N.C., 27, 43, 54–57, 218, 252, 258, 263

horse conch, 57, 101, 118, 136–37, 173, 187, 220–21
horses, 48, 71, 161
horseshoe crab, 103, 272
hurricanes, 27, 30–33, 114, 144; Fran, 30; Ian, 30, 32–33, 93, 151, 195, 205; Ida, 107

imperial Venus, 59
Indigenous artifacts, 256–57; arrowheads, 256–57; points, 256; pottery shards, 262
Isle of Palms, S.C., 63

Jacksonville, Fla., 74
Jekyll Island, Ga., 70–73, 140, 265
jellyfish, 170, 172
Jeremy Inlet, S.C., 64–65, 67
jetties, 136–37, 139–40
jewelbox, 246–47; leafy, 246–47; spiny, 246–47
John Pennekamp Coral Reef State Park, 202
Juno Beach, Fla., 74, 76–77, 140, 229
junonia, 93, 149–50, 152, 155, 213–15
Jupiter Beach, Fla., 76–77; Jupiter Dog Beach, 76

kayaking, 90
Keewaydin Island, Fla., 24, 88–92, 141, 149–52, 164, 214, 221
Key West, Fla., 79–81, 93, 178–79, 201, 261
Kiawah Island, S.C., 63
Kice Island, Fla., 86, 197
king tide, 24–25, 131; spring tide 24–25
king's crown, 156, 248
Kino sandals, 178–79
Kiser, Justin, 158–59
knobbed whelk, 237

lace murex, 242–43
leafy jewelbox, 246–47
Lido Key, Fla., 97–99, 214; South Lido Key, 97–98; South Lido Key Beach Park, 98
Lighthouse Beach (Sanibel, Fla.), 93–94, 96
lightning whelk, 237
lion's paw, 19, 55, 217
Litchfield, S.C., 58–59, 230
Little River, S.C., 58
Little St. Simon's Island, Ga., 70
live shelling, 172–76, 202
Loggerhead Marinelife Center, 76
Longboat Key, Fla., 203
Lover's Key, Fla., 92
Lowcountry, 62–64, 159

Marco Island, Fla., 22, 24–25, 85, 88–92, 140, 167, 197, 214, 245
megalodon, 44, 50, 252
mermaid's purse, 274
Miami, Fla., 77–78
Migratory Bird Treaty Act, 276
military artifacts, 258–59; bullet casings, 50
mineral oil, 188
mini shells, 198–99, 228
Mobile Bay, Ala., 104
moon phases, 23–26
moon snail, 63, 96, 231–32; Paul Newman moon snail, 231; shark's eye, 231
mosasaurus, 54
mosquitos, 193
murex, 242–44; apple, 242; Cabrit's, 243–44; giant Atlantic, 54, 244; lace, 242–43; rose, 89, 243
muriatic acid, 188–89
Myrtle Beach, S.C., 58–59, 115
Myrtle Beach Shark Teeth (Facebook), 207

National Park Service, 48
National Seashore, 48
Navarre Beach, Fla., 104–5; pier, 104–5
neap tide, 26

negative low tide, 24–26
New River Inlet, N.C., 50
night hunting, 146–48, 167, 171
No Natz, 194
North Myrtle Beach, S.C., 58
No-See-Ums, 192–94
nutmeg, 115, 241

Ocean Isle Beach, N.C., 142, 252, 263
Ocracoke Island, N.C., 47
octopus, 170
olive, 58–60, 98, 233; golden, 233
Onslow Beach, N.C., 50–52, 234, 252, 259
operculum, 275
Orlando, Fla., 121
Outer Banks, N.C., 47–49

Palm Beach County, Fla., 76–77, 216
Panama City, Fla., 104
paper nautilus, 212
Pass-A-Grille, Fla., 100–101, 121, 139
Paul Newman moon snail, 231
Pawley's Island, S.C., 58; Pawley's Island Gray Man, 59; Pawley's shell, 59
Pea Island, N.C., 47
Pensacola, Fla., 104
Perdido Key, Fla., 104
periostracum, 136, 186–87
plesiosaurus, 54
points, 256
Port St. Lucie, Fla., 74
Portsmouth Island, N.C., 47
Portuguese man o' war, 169–70
predators, 165–66
Prince Resort (S.C.), 58
purple ianthina, 212
pusher tide, 131–32, 136

queen conch, 82, 202–3

raking, 15, 125–27, 182
ram's horn, 8
ray mouth plate, 108
reading the beach, 113–16, 143
receding tide, 19
red lights, 175
red tide, 40, 144, 190–91
renourishment, 42–44, 54–56, 59, 168–69; dredging, 42; replenishment, 42; nourishment, 42
rivers, 157–59
rose murex, 89, 243
rose tellin, 89, 245
roseate spoonbill, 276

safety, 165–70
sailcat, 275
sand dollar, 70–72, 101, 155, 174, 263, 265–66
Sand Dollar Spit, 89
sandbars, 135, 168
Sanibel Island, Fla., 12, 27, 85, 93–96, 118, 145, 195, 213
Sarasota, Fla., 97, 99, 247
Savannah, Ga., 68
Savannah River, 68
scallop, 51, 74, 94, 172; flat, 55, 105, 161, 218–19; yellow, 277
Scotch bonnet, 14, 38, 53, 76, 114, 161, 216–17, 241
sea bean, 253–55; hamburger, 254; sea heart, 254
sea biscuit, 54–55, 57, 184–85, 263–64
sea foam, 31
sea glass, 260–62
sea heart, 254
Sea Island, Ga., 70
sea urchin, 263, 267–68
seahorse, 172
Shackleford Banks/Island, N.C., 47–48, 164, 224

shark teeth, 148, 251–52, 256; great white, 61, 252; megalodon, 44, 50, 252
sharks, 2, 168
shark's eye, 231
SharkToothShackSC, 158
She Sells Sea Shells, 37
shell beds/hash, 12–15
shell cleaning, 183–89
shell collection rules, 202–3
shell display, 189
Shell Island, Fla., 86, 132
shell washout, 114–15
Shellinators (Facebook), 205–6, 209
shelling grid, 122–23
shelling shoes, 32
Siesta Key, Fla., 97–99, 233
sifting, 125–27, 182
sink holes, 168
slipper shell, 185
Smathers Beach, Fla., 80
snorkeling, 181
Sozon's cone, 104
spiny jewelbox, 246–47
spiny oyster, 77
spring tide, 24–25
squid, 8
St. Andrews Beach Park, 71–72
St. George Island, Fla., 102
St. Mary's, Fla., 71
St. Petersburg, Fla., 100
St. Simon's Island, Ga., 70, 73
starfish, 172, 174, 269–70
sucker tide, 131–32
Sun Dial Beach Resort (Fla.), 94
sundial, 76, 229
sunray Venus, 137
sunrise tellin, 245
sunrises, 200–201
sunsets, 200–201
swash zone, 128–29, 130, 144

T. H. Stone Memorial St. Joseph Peninsula State Park, 102, 169
Tampa, Fla., 100, 121
Tarpon Springs, Fla., 100
tellin, 245; rose, 89, 245; sunrise, 245
Ten Thousand Islands, Fla., 18, 24, 85–87, 101, 151, 201, 206
Terramar Beach, Calif., 277
tests, 267–68
tidal pool, 136–39
tide chart, 17–20, 22–25; datum, 17
Tidetime.org, 17
Tigertail Beach, Fla., 89, 140, 245, 265; Tigertail Beach Park, 89
Topsail Island, N.C., 14, 52–53, 252
training your eye, 155–56
Treasure Island, Fla., 100
tree roots, 136
tropical storm, 27, 30–33
trough, 124
true tulip, 92, 238–40
tulip 87, 238–40; banded, 115, 238, 240, 275; true, 92, 238–40
tun, 51, 225–26
Turner Beach, Fla., 94, 96
Turtle Beach, Fla., 97
turtles, 202; nesting, 175
Tybee Island, Ga., 68–69, 139; lighthouse, 68

underwater viewing bucket, 182

vinegar soaking, 185–86
visibility, 22, 144–45
volute, 195
Vrbo, 55

water clarity, 22, 144–45
Watie's Island, S.C., 136
wave height, 31
weather, 34–35, 171

wedding shell, 195–96
wentletrap, 230
West End Beach (Dauphin Island, Ala.), 107
West Wind Inn (Fla.), 94
whelk, 61, 175, 236–37; channel, 237; knobbed, 237; lightning, 237
wind, 27–33
Windy.com, 33
Witherington, Blair and Dawn, 204
worm snail, 114
wrack line, 12–13

yellow scallop, 277

About the Author

Dr. Ashley Oliphant is a retired professor of English with teaching specialties in twentieth-century American literature, the works of Ernest Hemingway, literary modernism, and rhetoric and composition. Her passion for learning about the ocean prompted her to pull away from full-time academia after twenty years of service and focus instead on offering interactive shark tooth and seashell hunting workshops for children and adults all over the United States. In addition to delivering lectures about her other research interests, including the later life of the pirate Jean Laffite and the Bahamian fishing exploits of Hemingway, Oliphant also teaches shark tooth and shelling courses in Coastal Carolina University's Osher Lifelong Learning Institute, which allows her the chance to take beach hunting excursions with very enthusiastic students.

Oliphant is the author of six other books. Her doctoral dissertation, completed at the University of North Carolina at Greensboro in 2007, was titled "Hemingway's Mixed Drinks: An Examination of the Varied Representation of Alcohol Across the Author's Canon." It's available for free with a Google search for any readers who want to geek out with it.

Shark Tooth Hunting on the Carolina Coast, published by Pineapple Press in 2015, is the only color guide to fossil shark teeth found in the Carolinas.

It has sold more than twenty thousand copies and is regarded as required reading in the shark tooth and fossil hunting community.

Hemingway and Bimini: The Birth of Sport Fishing at "The End of the World" was published by Pineapple Press in 2017. It follows Hemingway's 1930s fishing adventures in Bimini, the westernmost Bahamian island, from 1935 to 1937 and his significant contribution to the founding of the International Game Fish Association. Oliphant's research for the book was completed at the John F. Kennedy Presidential Library in Boston on an Ernest Hemingway Research Grant and at the IGFA's headquarters in Dania Beach, Florida. Oliphant is a longtime member of the Hemingway Society and a contributor to its conferences and *The Hemingway Review*. She also regularly participates in the scholarly activities associated with Key West's Hemingway Days celebration every July.

Her fourth book, a comedic novel titled *In Search of Jimmy Buffett: A Key West Revival*, was released in April 2018 by Warren Publishing. It tells the story of Livie Green, an English professor at a rural North Carolina university who has a bit of a meltdown and moves to Key West in the middle of a semester to become a waitress in a bar. Having convinced herself that she has written the perfect Jimmy Buffett song, she spends her tropical nights waiting in his old haunts for one of his legendary surprise visits and the chance to meet her hero. After Buffett's untimely passing in 2023, the book now stands as a fitting tribute to the greatest hard-drinking calypso poet who ever lived.

In 2021 Oliphant coauthored a book with Beth Yarbrough, her mother, titled *Jean Laffite Revealed: Unraveling One of America's Longest Running Mysteries*. Published by the University of Louisiana at Lafayette Press, the book proves the New Orleans pirate Jean Laffite faked his death in the 1820s, hid in Cuba for a time, and then reentered the United States using an alias. By using primary archival documents and artifacts, the mother-daughter team was able to establish that Laffite ultimately landed in North Carolina and lived to be a ninety-six-year-old man without ever being caught.

In 2022, Warren Publishing released *Higher Education: Chronicles of a Dumpster Fire*, the irreverent prequel to *In Search of Jimmy Buffett*. In it, Oliphant explores all of the things going wrong at America's colleges and universities these days. After teaching for two decades and viewing academia's decline from the front seat, she had quite a few things she needed to say.

Oliphant is an animal welfare advocate in her local community. As the founder of the Humane Voters of Lincoln County, she spearheaded the successful movement to end the use of the gas chamber at her county shelter. She's also the longtime chairperson of the Lincoln County, North Carolina, Animal Services Advisory Board and has worked for years to help the shelter achieve and then maintain its No Kill designation.

In her spare time, Oliphant travels with her family (including her son Miller and her husband Chris) and floats in her swimming pool. She has two cats, Irish Kevin and Tuna, though Tuna likes her a whole lot more than Kevin does. Her lifelong dreams are to own a signed first edition of Hemingway's *The Old Man and the Sea* and to meet Willie Nelson.

If you're interested in scheduling Dr. Oliphant as a speaker for your school, library, museum, book club, shell club, summer camp, or organizational meeting, please send inquiries about dates and pricing to her team at professoroliphant@gmail.com.